HOW TO PUT YOUR ASSETS IN TRUST, EVEN IN WILLS!

Sadick H. Keshavjee, LLB (Hon.) Lon

Order this book online at www.trafford.com
or email orders@trafford.com

Most Trafford titles are also available at major online book retailers.

This booklet has been created for informational purposes only and does not contain a full
analysis of the law, nor does it constitute a legal opinion. Please contact us to schedule a
confidential consultation with one of our professionals

Printed in the United States of America.

ISBN: 978-1-4669-7183-7 (sc)

Trafford rev. 09/30/2013

 www.trafford.com

North America & international
toll-free: 1 888 232 4444 (USA & Canada)
fax: 812 355 4082

CONTENTS

WILLS

This book is dedicated to my late mother, late wife, and my immediate family Naveeda, Nadeem, and Alyssa, Nadeem's significant other.

SADICK H. KESHAVJEE

ACKNOWLEDGMENTS

As a past member of the worldwide association entitled the Society of Trust and Estates Practitioners. (STEP), I have quoted from their highly esteemed publications. They are the leading professional body for the trust and estate profession worldwide. This international body is run by David Harvey and his able team

I thank my friend Nadim Kurji a truly bright and enterprising young Ontario based lawyer for going through my manuscript, and providing some valuable input.

STEP members come from the legal, accountancy corporate administration banking financial planning insurance and related professions.

I have compiled my material on the international scene from the latest STEP Directory and Yearbooks.

E mail step@step.org
Website http://www.step.org

I have been an avid fan of Prof. Amyn Sajoo who is an authority on Islamic law at a prestigious

Canadian University as well as a consultant with the Institute of Ismaili studies in the UK. Most of my material on topical Islamic Law subjects is from this intellectual giant. His work can be accessed from www.iis.org

I thank the attorney General of Kenya, Hon. Mr. Amos Wako for kindly agreeing to do the forewords to my earlier editions, despite his busy schedule. Not only do I admire him for his intellectual prowess but also his efficacy as an Attorney General.

Shairose Remtulla an able certified paralegal currently working at a prestigious Canadian law firm has been ably editing my manuscript, despite her busy schedules as a mother, home maker and an employee.

I thank Kashfi and Faizan Manji my young and enterprising neighbors with transcribing and editing.

Last but not least I thank my daughter a graduate from Queens University in Political Science for assistance in editing this manuscript as well.

Any errors and omissions are wholly my responsibility, though.

A classic trust

A society matron placed an advertisement in the local newspaper offering to sell a brand new Cadillac in first class condition with low mileage for $50. Because nobody believed that it was a genuine offer it was some time before a buyer appeared. When one finally did he found that it was a real offer . . . . and with no strings attached. It seems that the lady had just became a widow and her late husband specified in his will that his Cadillac or the proceeds from the sale of the car were to go to his girlfriend, from a trust fund resulting from a will.

SUMMARY

I have tried to use plain English and explain technical words. I have also included a glossary of terms.

I have meanwhile used English precedents, which have persuasive authority in most countries which have had historical ties to England, subject to changes in the law since ties were broken.

I have not cluttered this booklet with citations of authorities but I have given all the authorities as footnotes so that someone who does want to concern themselves with them may do so.

In the first chapter I have indicated what a trust is, indicating advantages of a trust, showing what trusts cannot do and comparisons with other concepts as well as brief notes on formalities, management, registering and updating trusts.

In the next chapter I have compared Trust Law with other laws that impact it like Property Law, Contract Law, Family Law, Equity, Perpetuities and Accumulations as well as Succession Law. In the next chapter I have covered the topic on the need for certainty in the formulation of a Trust.

Then I give a brief background to various types of Trusts like Constructive Trusts, Discretionary & Protective Trusts Secret Trusts & Trusts resulting from Mutual (Chap. 6) and Resulting Trusts.

The important topic—Charitable Trusts are then covered. This includes notes on the essentials of a Charity and then trusts for the relief of poverty. Educational Trusts, Religious Trusts and Trusts for Sports and Recreation.

The next few chapters deal with the administrative aspects of Trusts like Appointment, Retirement and Removal of Trustees, Powers of Trustees and Investment Duties.

The next chapter has a discussion on Trust Corporations followed by a sample Trust.

I have included a Glossary of terms.

The international scene is discussed followed by the law reform scene in Canada.

I have finally discussed dispute resolution with particular reference to trusts and Estates.

CHAPTER 1

WHAT IS A TRUST

More than a 100 years ago, Oliver Wendell Holmes said "put not your trust in money, but put your money in trust.

Most people understand the importance of wills but comparatively few know anything about trusts. In this case ignorance is not bliss.

A trust is an arrangement in which one person transfers his property to a second person for the benefit of a third person. The person to whom the assets belong creating the trust is called the Grantor. The person holding legal title to the trust property is the trustee and the person for whose benefit the trust is created is called the beneficiary. (The same person can be the grantor, trustee, and beneficiary all at the same time).

Trusts offer something for everyone. For example, It can provide protection for everyone. It can provide protection for a child who may be handicapped or a relative who is disabled.

Living (or Inter vivos) trusts are extremely flexible. They therefore offer the most benefit for the greatest number of people.

You create a trust during your lifetime and fund it with most of your assets. Once in the trust your money and property are under the control of the trustee. That should not, however, bother you. You can choose to be the initial trustee of your own trust and therefore you remain in control.

You can at any time take money or property out of the trust, put More into it, change it completely revoke it, or change the beneficiaries.

You remain in control as long as you wish or until your death when the person you have named as your successor trustee takes over.

WHAT ARE THE ADVANTAGES OF A TRUST

1. You can avoid probate with regard to the property that you put in trust.

   a) Takes less time.
      Probate like most court proceedings can take years. With a trust the property passes on to your named beneficiaries very soon.
   b) Ensures privacy
      Probate records are public. Anyone can examine your personal information. Trusts

on the other hand are completely private. No one can find out what you or who you are leaving your assets to.

c) Probate costs can be very high.
There would be a saving even if part of your assets are in trust. This is because most of the executors work will have been completed when the trust was established. Also, generally, the smaller the estate to be probated the lower the legal fees and court charges.

d) Generally trusts are more difficult to contest than wills.
When a will is contested, the assets cannot be disturbed until the claim is resolved. This encourages litigation as prospective plaintiffs know that beneficiaries would often prefer to settle rather than face long delays.

2. Prevents problems with disability
A very important but often ignored advantage of a trust is to ensure that someone will be available to handle your financial and legal affairs if serious illness renders you incapable of handling your affairs for yourself.
If your assets were owned by a trust your trustee would continue to manage these assets despite your disability.

3. Protects heirs inheritance
You could stipulate that your adult child not receive his/her inheritance till they

6

reach 25. Also, thereafter arrangements can be made to transfer the principal over a specified period of time—say in installments at 2 year intervals.

4. You could provide for a handicapped loved one.

Suppose you are in a situation where you are caring for a handicapped child or other family member or even a friend who is unable to work or otherwise handle his or her own affairs. What will happen to that person when you die? Instead of having your assets transferred on your death, you could leave them in trust with instructions that the income, principal or both be used for that individuals benefit. A successor trustee also named in the trust document who may be a relative, friend or even a trust corporation would continue to manage the funds. Provision can be made for the assets to be distributed to your remaining beneficiaries after the handicapped person died.

To avoid probate, your trust must be created and your assets transferred into it before you die.

WHAT CAN'T TRUSTS DO?

Trusts do not always protect assets from creditors. If you put assets in trust to avoid creditors contemplating bankruptcy proceedings, this kind of transfer can be held to be void.

Trusts do not always eliminate the need for wills and probate. There may be assets that were outside the trust, requiring probate. This may include certain literary rights, (royalties from a book) or royalties from music you might have had a tape or record made of.

In a will you can put in a "blanket clause" (standard) providing for the "residue" (what's left in the estate) of your estate to be given to certain named beneficiary/ies. This will deal with assets that you might have left out because you were unaware of. Examples would be money owing to you, a valid legal claim against someone or royalties from a book that you had just written.

It is worthwhile to have a will for assets that have been left out of a trust.

If you have a will, a personal guardian can be named for your minor children. This cannot be done in a trust.

WHAT TAKES PRECEDENCE—A TRUST OR A WILL?

You should not expect to leave in a will property that you have already transferred to a trust. The reason is that a trust takes precedence over the will because ownership of the asset was immediately transferred when the trust was established.

A Will only becomes operative on the death of a person.

HOW DO TRUSTS COMPARE WITH JOINT OWNERSHIP

Many married couples hold property as joint owners (as joint tenants—JIT). This is a good way to avoid probate as the balance of property is easily transferred to the surviving spouse.

There are pitfalls, however in putting property in joint tenancy with other beneficiaries for the following reasons:

One you may lose control of your property if your joint owner does not agree with your plans e.g. to sell or mortgage the property. You could also lose the property to a creditor of your joint owner.

And secondly Joint ownership is not appropriate for all property e. g. a motor car or a painting.

NOMINATION OF PROPERTY HELD BY A MEMBER OF A CO-OPERATIVE SOCIETY VS A TRUST

Generally a "nomination" (entry of the name of a beneficiary in the books of a co-operative society) of a dwelling home or any other asset has precedence over a will or trust.

Therefore if you have nominated, say, your son in the co-operative society books, you cannot then will it to your wife.

WHAT DO YOU HAVE TO CONSIDER WHEN SELECTING A TRUSTEE

A trust can be operated by up to 4 trustees. An alternative would be to appoint a trust corporation.

Make sure that the trustee has agreed to act. This is why appointing more than one is a good idea.

You can allow your trustee to name his or her successor. Usually, however, the trustee in the deceased trustees will becomes the substitute trustee of the testator on the passing off of the named trustee.

You can be your own trustee.

Be certain that a prospective trustee realises his rights and obligations. He/she is liable to serious repercussions if the trust is not managed properly, there is conflict of interest, or he obtains an undisclosed personal gain.

Whether a trustee is compensated for his or her services is strictly a matter of agreement between the grantor and the trustee. A trust corporation, or lawyer however is expected be remunerated.

WHAT PROPERTY SHOULD BE PUT INTO A TRUST

Generally most property can be put in a trust. The following checklist would prove useful.

AEROPLANES
ANTIQUES
ARTWORK
COPYRIGHT
TRADEMARKS
PATENTS
BOAT
BUSINESS INTERESTS
HOLIDAY HOMES
PERSONAL RESIDENCES
SHARES OR STOCKS IN A COMPANY (PRIVATE OR PUBLIC)
BONDS AND TREASURY BILLS
LAND, BUILDINGS ETC.
SAVINGS ACCOUNT
DEBTS DUE
CASH
LIFE INSURANCE

The following asset is best left out of the trust

Personal checking accounts

WHAT ARE THE FORMALITIES IN TRANSFERRING PROPERTY

Land, buildings, houses etc., are transferred by deed.

Bearer securities and chattels are transferred by a sale agreement.

Stocks and bonds are transferred by delivery to a stock broker to transfer to the trust.

HOW DOES ONE MANAGE THE TRUST PROPERTY

Apart from preparing the trust document and transferring your assets to it you have to:

1. Keep simple records to show:

   - All property transferred to and from the trust.
   - All income earned by the trust.
   - All expenses incurred and payments made by the trust.

2. Operate a separate bank account for the trust

   - It should read; "John Ouma trust by David Otieno trustee"

> ➤ This signing format should be used on all documents when you act on behalf of the trust.

3. Insure trust property

WHAT RIGHTS DO THE TRUSTEES HAVE?

Because during your lifetime you are trustee you can:

1. Sell or gift property in the trust.
2. Mortgage or borrow against the trust property.
3. Add property to the trust.
4. Retransfer to yourself property contained in the trust.
5. Change beneficiaries.
6. No creditor of a beneficiary can attach the interest of the beneficiary until it passes to the beneficiary.
7. Since the trustee only holds title to the trust assets on behalf of the grantor, the trust property is safe from creditors of the trustee.

The trustee has the power to: Manage, sell, encumber, pledge, lease or invest the trust property, as long as he/she does not make a personal profit from this.

HOW DO YOU NAME BENEFICIARIES

As with a will, you designate specific property to specific beneficiaries, or alternatively you may leave beneficiaries a set percentage or all of the property in the trust.

Examples:

If to the guardian of a minor: "To Fredick Ngombo as a guardian of Stephen Ondik, a minor child."

If two or more beneficiaries (specific property): "To Rachel Smith and John Brown in equal shares, as their sole separate property."

You can also allow for contingencies: "In the event my son John shall predecease me, I leave his shares to his then surviving children equally"

REGISTERING THE TRUST

If the trust is to hold land and buildings (real estate) it will be necessary to register the trust in the lands office.

WHEN DO YOU UPDATE TRUSTS (AND EVEN WILLS)

How often should you review your trust? At least once a year is a good safe bet.

What kind of events would trigger the need for a change?

1. Your divorce.

   ➤ You will most likely not want your former spouse continuing as trustee or beneficiary.

2. You remarry.

   ➤ The same would apply and you may want to add your spouse to your trust arrangement.

3. A beneficiary or trustee passes away (or his or her alternate dies)

4. You dispose of or acquire new assets or your assets change in value.

5. You change your mind about when, say a grandchild should receive a benefit.

   ➤ You might want him to receive the capital at age 25 instead of 30.

6. The status of a beneficiary changes.

   ➤ One of your beneficiaries might win a lottery and you may want to decrease that persons share.

7. Changed circumstances of your trustee.

➢ You might decide to change the trustee because your original choice may not be the best one.

8. A trust may also cease to operate where there is no more property in the trust

Modification of the trust may therefore involve:

1. Change of trustee.
2. Addition or deletion of property.
3. Change of beneficiaries.
4. Change of trust terms.

CHAPTER 2

CONCEPTS & PRINCIPLES

Trust Law is impacted upon by other laws.

It might be worthwhile, therefore at this stage, to discuss legal principles in outline of other aspects of law to put things in proper perspective. Examples are the Law of property {including co-ownership}, the Principles of Equity, Succession, Contract and Family Law.

PROPERTY LAW (Property that is capable of ownership). There are two types of property:

1. Personal Property (Personalty)
2. Real Property (Realty)

There are 3 types of Personal Property:

A. Chose in possession—these are tangible things other than land.

  ➤ Examples are cars, furniture, clothes etc.

B. Chose in action—these are things you cannot hold (intangible).

➢ Examples are debts, shares, trademarks, copyrights, patents etc.

C. Leaseholds—having a lease on property in return for payment of, say, rent.

Realty is freehold land. This includes "pastures" wood, marshes, castles, houses and other buildings. It includes not only buildings on soil but fixtures.

A contract for the sale or other disposition of an interest in land has to be evidenced in writing.

CO-OWNERSHIP OF LAND

Where two or more persons hold interests in the land at the same time, they hold the interests as co-owners either as:

1. Joint Tenancies (JT) or
2. Tenancies In Common (T.I.C)—tenancy here implies 'ownership'.

In a joint tenancy, no one joint tenant owns an identifiable portion of the whole land even though each has an interest that is subject to the joint tenancy by will nor can he sell it. No single JT can identify for himself or herself his or her own share or portion.

Each Joint Tenant is entitled to possession of every part of the land and they must acquire their title at the same time and under the same document. One can therefore leave a property to two or more persons "as joint tenants". When one JT dies, the property passes on to the other JT irrespective of what a Will stipulates.

Tenancies In Common (TIC). Each TIC can hold a "divided" share in a land especially where land is purchased in unequal shares. A TIC can dispose of his or her share in a will.

CONTRACT LAW

A contract is an agreement that the law will enforce. An agreement is essential in addition to other requirements.

There must be an "offer and there must be an "acceptance". This is the core of a contract and comprise of the first two elements.

Both parties must contribute something of value to the bargain e.g. money, work, goods etc.—this is termed 'consideration' and is the third element.

Fourthly the parties must intend to be legally bound.

And on the other hand, a social agreement e.g. to "date" a person is not a legally binding contract. If someone breaks his promise to keep the "date" he is not legally bound.

The fifth element of a contract is that both parties must be able to enter into the contract. A mentally disordered person, a drunk, a person under 18 and someone under the influence of drugs cannot enter into a valid contract. The term usually given to this is "capacity".

Contracts can be oral or in writing. Contracts relating to land, however, have to be in writing. As long as there is consideration, one can make a legally binding contract to make a Will, to benefit the other party to the contract.

FAMILY LAW

As the name implies, this includes Marriage, Adoption of Children etc.

What is marriage?—It is the voluntary union for life of one man and one woman to the exclusion of all others. "Marriage" shares some similarities with a contractual relationship.

Both parties must have "Capacity" to contract a valid marriage and all the necessary formalities must be completed. The married couple have certain rights to 'consortium' (mutual support and sharing) examples are, the right to occupy a matrimonial home, rights to reasonable sexual intercourse, the right to use the husband surname etc. In Contract Law, it is presumed that both parties do not intend to create legal relations (unless evidence can show otherwise). The husband has the duty in common law to maintain the children of the relationship. This relationship can end either by nullity, divorce or judicial separation.

During marriage, spouses have a mutual obligation to provide financial support for each other. On divorce, the burden shifts to one spouse depending on the arrangements made by the court or by the parties themselves. Further changes will be made in relation to property and financial provisions can be ordered in favour of any children.

EQUITY

Equity primarily means fairness or natural justice. It is a fresh body of rules by the side of the original law, founded on distinct principles and claiming to the law by virtue of a superior sanctity inherent in these principles.

There were two main developments in the common Law in England in the early centuries. One was the Provision of Oxford (1258) which had the effect of severely restricting the writ (A document in the crowns name commanding the person to whom it is addressed to do or forbear from doing some act) that could be issued by the "royal" courts in existence at that time. The second development was the Statute of Westminster which provided that new writs could only be issued which were similar to those in existence before the Provisions of Oxford.

The fact that Common Law required the right form of action that one could only obtain damages and the fact that people "in high places" could defy the law was of concern to the King. More so as he was considered the "Fountain of Justice". The King delegated these matters to the Chancellor who was thought to be the "The Keeper of the Kings Conscience". He in turn set up Chancery Courts which operated in different ways from the common Law Courts. If the Chancellor was satisfied after persistent questioning by him that the defendant had done wrong and that his conscience was burdened by guilt, he would order the defendant to make good his wrong and so clear his conscience.

This type of justice which had no binding rules became known as Equity. Each Chancellor was able to give judgment based on his own conscience and this resulted in the expression that "Equity varies with the length of the Chancellors foot".

With the JUDICATURE ACTS of 1873-77, the separate systems were fused, the Chancery Courts being abolished. The Common Law remedies of damages and equitable remedies of injunction and specific performance could now be obtained from the same court.

Therefore, in a matter like, say, a nuisance claim' damages' and an 'injunction' could be sought from the same court. Over a period of time, however, Equity built up its own series of rules and precedents. The Maxims ("concise truths") of Equity cover the general principles or guidelines which evolved in the Courts of Chancery.

Well known examples of maxims of Equity:

i. Equity will not suffer a wrong to without a remedy
   A Plaintiff may be granted a temporary injunction to preserve his right until the trial because the common law remedy of damages would be inadequate and which

is, in any case, only available after end of the trial.

ii. _He who comes to equity must come with clean hands_
A Plaintiff who seeks equitable relief must have acted fairly towards the defendant. A Tenant cannot get specific performance of a contract for a lease if he has already breached his obligations.

iii. _Equity imputes an intention to fulfil an obligation_
Where a person is obliged to do some act, and does some other act which could be regarded as a performance of it, then it will be so regarded in Equity. If a debtor leaves a legacy to his creditor of an amount equal to or greater than the debt, this is presumed to be a repayment of the debt.

iv. _Equity regards as done that which ought to be done_
A contract relating to land is specifically enforceable (to force someone to act on a matter) if there is writing or part performance.

v. _Equity is equality_
Where two or more persons are entitled to an interest in the same property in a will, then

the principles of Equity is equal division, if there is no good reason for any other basis for division.

vi. _Equity looks at the intent rather than the form_
A Trust may be created although the word "Trust" has not been used in a Will.

THE RULE AGAINST PERPETUITIES

Perpetuities is defined as a disposition of property by which its" absolute vesting" (effective right to possession) is postponed indefinitely.

Perpetuities are contrary to the policy of the law as it "ties up" property and prevents its free alienation (the power to dispose of an interest).

This rule came about in England in the 17th century because rich families would keep land from generation to generation within the family. This was considered against public policy.

The rule therefore evolved so that the vesting (right to possession) of an interest should not be unreasonably postponed.

The rule therefore requires that every "estate" (interest in land) or "interest" (rights, titles, interest) must be bound to vest, and if at all, not less than 21 years after the ending of some life in being at the date, when the instrument creating such estate or interest takes effect.

1. The rule dates back to 1682[1]. It stated that, "A grant or other limitation of any estate or interest to take effect in possession or enjoyment at a future time, and which is not, from the time of its creation, a vested estate or interest, will be void. (ab initio) (from the beginning) if at the time when the instrument containing the limitation takes effect, there is a possibility that the estate or interest limited will not vest within the period of a life or lives then in being or within a further period of 21 years thereafter."

The Perpetuities and Accumulations Act 1964[2] enables (but does not compel) a period not exceeding 80 years to be fixed as the relevant period by a person, in any instrument by which any disposition is made.

A Will takes effect at the death of the Testator.

Hence, the devise or bequest will be void if it does not necessarily vest within 21 years from the

---

[1]   DUKE OF NORFOLKS CASE 1683—2 SWAN 454
[2]   S. 1(1)

26

termination of any life in being at the testator's death[3].

For the purpose of the rule, a child "en ventre sa mere" (of a pregnant mother) who is subsequently born, is considered as a life in being at the testators death.

Before the 1964 Act, it had always been assumed in the application of the rule that a woman, no matter how old she was, was capable of bearing a child[4].

After the Act, however, it must be presumed in any perpetuity matter, that a male can beget a child when he is 14 and over, and that a female can bear a child age 12-55.

When this applies to gifts to a class of persons (a particular group of people) not only must the persons to take the gifts be ascertained, but also the amount of the interest of each party taking must be determined within the perpetuity period[5].

CONDITIONS RESTRAINING ALIENATION

Where a disposition of a property is subject to a condition or limitation, absolutely restraining

[3] RE WILMER'S TRUSTS (1903) 2 CH. 411
[4] RE DAWSON'S (1888) 39 CH D 155
[5] S. 4 PERPETUITIES AND ACCUMULATIONS ACT 1964

the beneficiary or any person claiming under him/her from charging or disposing of his interest in the property the condition or limitation is void.

This rule again does not apply to a disposition for charitable purposes.

RESTRICTIONS REPUGNANT TO INTEREST

Where a disposition creates an interest absolutely in favor of any person but the term of the disposition directs that the interest shall be applied or enjoyed by him in a particular manner, he is entitled to receive and dispose of the interest as if there were no such direction.

INTERVIVOS TRANSFERS

Unlike a Will, an "Inter Vivos" (During life: between living persons) disposition (disposal, distribution) of property takes effect immediately.

Of course, an inter vivos disposition can take place conditional upon the occurrence of an event other than the grantors own death.

If, on the other hand, the condition is that the deed shall take effect only on the death of the grantor, the document is a Will (if property signed and witnessed).

28

In an old case[6], the deceased during his lifetime executed three deeds of gift (a gift evidenced in writing "signed", sealed and delivered).

These documents contained a clause directing that it was not to take effect until after his death. They were signed and witnessed as Wills should have been. The court held that the three deeds of gift together contained the Will of the deceased and granted probate of them.

SUCCESSION LAW refers to the transmission of property on the death of a person.

If one makes a will, then property devolves on a person or persons as directed in the will. The will has to be validly prepared, signed and witnessed.

The will also appoints executors, trustees and even guardians of children.

If there is no will or certain dispositions in a will are held to be invalid then "Intestate" Succession Law takes effect and the person dies "intestate" i.e. without a will with regard to the whole estate or for that portion of the estate found to be "intestate".

IN THE GOODS OF MORGAN (1866) LRIP & D 214

If someone dies intestate, the law stipulates how the estate is to be distributed dependant on, if there was a spouse and/or children,

If insufficient provision is made for a spouse or dependant then the "family provisions" are invoked, whereby a spouse or dependent, can apply to the courts for adequate provision depending on the circumstances of the case.

The subject of succession law does not only involve the formalities of making a will. It involves the capacity of the parties who make a will, revocation, alteration and revival of wills, types of dispositions and their failure. Family provisions and intestacy law which are covered by the act are vast issues to be considered.

The matter of personal representatives are covered as well. The act contains detailed provisions as to the formalities of applying for probate of a will or applying for letters of administration if there is no will.

CHAPTER 3

CERTAINTY

WHAT IS CERTAINTY IN TRUST?

There is a basic, long established rule about trusts that are non-charitable and that is it must be certain i.e. certain with regard to the intention of the settler, the subject matter of the property and the objects.

The judgment in a 19th Century case contains the classic formulation. Lord Langdale stated when defining "certainty".[7]

> "If the words were so used, that upon the whole they ought to be construed as imperative, secondly if the subject matter of the recommendation or will be certain, thirdly if the objects or persons intended to have the benefit of the recommendation be certain."

To prove that a settlers intention was a legal and not a moral obligation one only had to prove it according to the ordinary civil standard (

---

[7]   KNIGHT v KNIGHT (1840) 3 BEAV. 148; 9 LJ Ch 354

i.e. on a "Balance of Probability") and not the strict standard as is required to prove an issue in a criminal case (i.e. "Beyond a Reasonable Doubt").[8]

In a decided case a testator left his property "Unto and to the absolute use of my wife in full confidence that she will do what is right as to the disposal thereof between my children".

These words were not held to be imperative, they did not create a trust for the children and they went to the wife absolutely.[9]

"HOPE" "CONFIDENCE", "DESIRE" OR "BELIEF" NO HELP

"PRECATORY WORDS" expressing hope, confidence, belief or desire indicate an intention to rely on the conscience of the recipient of the property and cannot be a legally enforceable obligation.

HISTORY OF DEALING A HELP

In addition to words used by the settler, consideration can also be given to other factors such as the type of relationship between the parties and the history of dealings between them.

---

[8] RE SNOWDEN (DECEASED) 1979 Ch 528; (1977) 2WLR 654
[9] RE ADAMS & THE KENSINGTON VESTRY (1884) 27 Ch D. 394; 54L.J. Ch 87

32

In a decided case[10] shortly after a Mr. Constance separated from his wife, he took up with Mrs. Paul and they cohabited. Mr. Constance and Mrs. Paul opened a joint bank account into which C puts £ 950 initially which he had received as damages for personal injuries.

Both of them drew money from the account. Mr. Constance told Mrs. Paul before and after the initial sum was deposited "This money is as much yours as mine". Mr. Constance then died without a will and his wife closed the account and Mrs. Paul claimed the money. The words often used by Mr. Constance were sufficient to constitute a declaration of trust, in favour of Mrs. Paul and it was held that she was entitled to the money.

WORDS PREVIOUSLY USED ARE A HELP

Where a form of words previously used, were held in a decided case to create a trust were used again it was held to create a trust.[11] The case where this rule resulted was criticized because each case must be decided upon its own facts.

---

[10]   PAUL v CONSTANCE 1977 1 WLR 527; M & B (T) p 85
[11]   RE STEELES WILL TRUST (1948) Ch 603 (1948) LJR 1888

CERTAINTY OF SUBJECT MATTER

What is certainty of subject matter?

There are two types of uncertainty

1. As to the amount of property to which the trust obligation refers.

In such a case[12], the transferee of the property takes it absolutely. In a decided case a settler left her estate to A for his own use and benefit "As I have full confidence in him that if he should die without lawful issue, he will, after providing for his widow during his life, leave the bulk of my residuary estate . . .".

As the subject matter of trust was not clearly designated, no trust had been created and A took the property absolutely.

The following words have been held to be unclear resulting in failure of the trust:

"or such parts of my estate as she shall not have sold";

"anything that is left":

---

[12]   PALMER v SIMMONDS (1854) 2 DREW 221, 2 WR 313

34

"the remaining part of what is left"; or

"all my other houses".

> 2. *As to the beneficial share of each of a member of beneficiaries, in which case the transferee holds the property on behalf of the settler[13].*

In a decided case[14], a settler provided for his daughter to receive a "reasonable" income and on a question of whether the direction was void for uncertainty, the context of the gift suggested an objective estimation of what "reasonable income is". It was held to be a valid gift, because a third party could gauge what "reasonable" income was.

In a 1789 case[15], a testatrix left her husband £300 for his sole use "and at his death, the remaining part of what is left & he does not want for his own wants & use to be divided between . . .". It was held that no trust was created because of uncertainty as to what would be left over.

Uncertainty as to the precise amount of property subjected to a secret trust or a trust arising under mutual wills has not proved inval.id. Thus if the

---

[13]   BOYCE v BOYCE (1849) 16 SIM 476
[14]   SPRANGE v BERNARD (1789) 2 BRO. CC 585; 29ER 320
[15]   SPRANGE v BERNARD (1789) 2 BRO. CC 585; 29ER 320

precise amount of property that a person puts into secret trust in a single will or the amount of property in mutual wills is not clear, the gift does not become invalid. (For secret trusts and mutual wills see "A background to wills by the author").

In such cases a trust obligation can be in suspense during someone's lifetime[16].

CERTAINTY OF OBJECTS

The objects or beneficiaries must be certain. If the beneficiaries are uncertain but the intention and subject matter certain the subject matter of the trust will be held in trust for the settlor or his estate.

One must then apply the relevant test for certainty of objects. This is important for courts in deciding on the administration of the trust or power. In a discretionary trust, one must be able to say with certainty whether any given individual is or is not a member of the class.

In the case of fixed trusts, it must possible to draw up a complete list of beneficiaries.

---

[16]   OTTAWAY v NORMAN (1972) Ch 698; (1972) 2WLR 50

36

None of the above should fail simply because it is not known where a particular beneficiary is, or whether he is still alive.

In addition to the requirements of certainty discretionary trusts must also be "administratively workable". This notion was introduced obiter by Lord Wilberforce in a 1970 case[17] and later applied in another case in 1985[18] to invalidate a trust for "Inhabitants of West Yorkshire".

Also if a power was conferred in a way that prevented any rational exercise it would never be validly exercised. Such a power would be void as being capriciously exercised[19].

[17]   MC PHAIL v DOULTON (1970) 2 WLR 1110
[18]   RV DISTRICT AUDITOR EXP WEST YORKSHIRE MCC
[19]   RE MANISTRYS SETTLEMENT (1974) Ch 17 (1973) 3WLR

CHAPTER 4

CONSTRUCTIVE TRUSTS

WHAT ARE THEY?

Generally, Constructive Trusts cover so many situations that to give a precise definition would not cover all situations. A 1967 case[20] defines it as "a trust which is imposed by equity in order to satisfy the demands of justice and good conscience without reference to any express or presumed intention of the parties".

NEW MODEL CONSTRUCTIVE TRUSTS

In many American jurisdictions, the constructive trust is seen as a remedy so as to return property and thereby prevent unjust enrichment that would be possible under normal circumstances.

In England, the new model "constructive trust" is similar to the American one but has been imposed in a much more discretionary manner, by the Courts.

38

Lord Denning in England in a 1972 case[21] aptly defines it as "A trust imposed by law whenever justice and good conscience requires it. It is a liberal process, founded on large principles of equity—it is an equitable remedy by which the court can enable an aggrieved party to obtain restitution".

THE DENNING CASES

The facts of a 1975 case[22] were that a couple lived together intending to marry. They had two children by the time of separation. When they had purchased a joint home, the man told the woman that the house would be their home but that it would have to be conveyed into his name alone as she was still under the age of majority being 21. In actual fact she had turned 21 by the time of the conveyance but the man still conveyed it to his name as the question of age had been used as an excuse to avoid using joint names. She made no financial contributions but did heavy work in the house and garden. She eventually made a claim in the courts and it was held that the woman would take a beneficial interest because the man's conduct was inequitable in denying her a share.

---

[21] HUSSEY v PALMER (1972) 1 W.L.R. 1286
[22] EVES v EVES (1975) 1 WLR 1388; (1975) 3 ALL ER 768

In another case[23], the wife contributed 4/5 of the price of a matrimonial home and the husband 1/5. The house was bought in the husband's name. The wife also transferred £40000 to the husband to save estate duty and £20000 to enable him to become a member of the prestigious "LLOYDS" of London. It was held by the court of appeal that the sum of £40000 and £20000 were held for the wife (on constructive trust) and the proceeds of sale of the house were divided 3/4 to the wife and 1/4 to the husband.

In another of the "Denning Cases" of 1972[24] a man and his mistress acquired a property by their joint efforts. The High Court, on a claim being made by the mistress, found that the mistress had contributed 1/12 of her property and was awarded 1/12. She appealed and got 1/3 of the proceeds.

Lord Denning thus produced results which were considered "fair" rather than following legal precedents and authorities. In fact Lord Denning was even castigated by the House of Lords for this.

The Denning cases also covered the protection of what were "contractual licensees". In a 1972 case[25], Mrs. Evans was the widow of an employee

---

[23]   HASELTINE v HASELTINE (1971)

[24]   COOKE v HEAD (1972) 1 W.L.R. 518

[25]   BINIONS v EVANS (1972) Ch 359 (1972) 2 W.L.R. 729 (1972) 2 ALL ER 70

of a housing estate. In 1968, the estate made an agreement with her under which she would be allowed to live in a cottage free of rent and rates for the rest of her life. She had, as part of the arrangement, undertaken to keep the cottage in a good state of repair.

Two years later, the estate sold the cottage to a Mr. Binion. The sale agreement clearly stipulated the fact that Mrs. Evans by a was a life tenant and the purchase price paid by Mr. Binion was reduced accordingly.

To Mrs. Evans surprise and dismay Mr. Binion soon thereafter claimed possession of the cottage. Lord Denning held that the purchaser was bound by Mrs. Evans "contractual license" and by a "constructive trust" in her favour. Despite the obvious Justice of the case this is not free from difficulty based on legal principles and it was thought that only after judicial dexterity by Lord Denning that the "Law is what it ought to be".

In another of Denning's contractual licensee cases decided in 1976[26], a holding company purchased land, the title to which was put in the name of a subsidiary company. By contract between them, the holding company remained in

---

26   DHN FOOD DISTRIBUTORS v LONDON BOROUGH OF TOWER HAMLETS (1976) 1 W.L.R. 852; 120 SJ 215

possession of the land and traded there. Upon a compulsory purchase order (CPO) being made by the authorities, the subsidiary was compensated for the value of the land (and not the holding company) for "disturbance". The holding company was held by the court of appeal to have had a sufficient interest to enable it to receive the compensation.

In a 1970 case[27] the wife had purchased a cottage in her name with her own funds. The husband had made improvements to it, which he valued at £723 and he later claimed that this improved the value of the house by £1000.

It was held after a claim having been made by the husband in the court, that the husband had acquired no rights as a result of his work and that there was a presumption of "advancement" (donation) by him to his wife.

In another case[28], a husband and wife purchased a matrimonial home in 1951 for £2965 in the husband's name. The purchase money was raised by a mortgage in his name and a loan from his employers. The wife paid £220 from her own savings to furnish and lay a new lawn.

---

[27]   PETTITT v PETTITT (1970 AC777); 1969 2 W.L.R. 966; (1969) 2 ALL ER 385
[28]   GISSING v GISSING (1971) AC. 886; (1970) 3 W.L.R. 255; (1970) 2 ALL ER 780

In 1961 the husband left the wife for another woman with whom he set up a home. At the time he said to the wife (according to her version of the evidence) "The house is yours" while he continued to pay the various outgoings. The couple divorced in 1966.

In subsequent proceedings, the High Court held that the husband was the sale owner and the court of appeal reversed the High Court decision.

On appeal to the House of Lords it was held that the wife did not have any beneficial interest in the house as she had made no contribution to the acquisition of the matrimonial home. Mr. Denning, was therefore overruled in the House of Lords.

In 1984[29] D (Defendant) left home in 1961 and started living with P (Plaintiff), having fallen in love with her. She was a 20 year old girl who had a job as a tailor at £12 per week. This relationship lasted for 19 years and P & D never married.

In 1963 P & D moved to a house which D purchased in his name. P had her second child in 1963 and until 1975 she did not earn as she had to stay at home to look after the children.

---

29   BURNS v BURNS (1984) Ch 317; (1984) 2 W.L.R. 582; (1984) ALL ER 244 CA

When she did earn there was no distinction between her own earnings and the housekeeping money D gave her. Unfortunately this 19 year affair ended and P was forced to leave the house in 1980. She brought an action claiming a beneficial interest in the house having contributed to the household for 19 years.

It was held on appeal that there was no evidence that P had made any contribution, directly or indirectly to the purchase of the house nor was there any intention all along this relationship that P would have a beneficial interest. Despite the obvious injustice of the case, the decision was based; on authoritative legal principles.

TIDE MOVES IN DENNING'S FAVOUR

In a 1986 case P (Plaintiff) who had split from her husband commenced cohabiting with D (Defendant). Although D intended to live permanently with P, he bought the house in the joint names of himself and of his brother and excluded P from holding a legal interest in the property. D explained to P that it was not wise to include her name on the title deeds of the property as this might adversely affect P's claim against her husband for matrimonial relief.

44

Even though Ps name was not on the title deeds she made substantial contributions to the co-habitation expenses by paying home-keeping expenses out of her earnings. Indirectly her contribution assisted in paying the mortgage payments.

It was held that P acted to her detriment in providing financial contributions towards housekeeping in the belief that she would acquire a beneficial interest in the house and she obtained a share in the house.

LIMITS TO THE "DENNING CASES" SET BY THE HOUSE OF LORDS

In a leading 1990 case[30] the husband had provided (from a trust fund of which he was a beneficiary), the purchase money for the matrimonial home. He had also arranged overdraft facilities from his bank to cover substantial renovation work that was done on the premises. The loan was secured by a charge on the house. The wife, though not having contributed financially towards the acquisition of the house had performed renovation work in the house. The husband then left the house, stopped making

---

[30]   LLYODS BANK v ROSSET (1990)

payments and did not contest the banks claim for repossession of the house.

The wife resisted the banks attempts at repossession arguing that she was entitled to a beneficial interest under a constructive trust, because of the renovation work done by her. The matter went up to the House of Lords who rejected the wife's claim.

In another case[31] substantial renovation work was done by an unemployed man, in return for board and lodging. It was held that no common interest was established, when the man applied to court claiming a beneficial interest in the property.

In yet another recent case[32], it was established that money provided by a mother-in-law for home improvements was considered to be a loan to her daughter-in-law and so she was held not to have a beneficial interest

The principle was laid in these cases that the mere fact that one person has expended money or labor on another person's property, does not by itself give the first person an interest in the property of the other person.

---

[31]   THOMAS v FULLER-BROWN (1988)
[32]   SPENCE v BROWN

For the claimant to succeed in such a situation, it would be necessary to show either an express agreement between the parties or a common intention to be inferred from all the circumstances of the case.

WHAT ABOUT JOINT TENANTS?

Generally a Joint Tenant becomes entitled under common law principles to the whole legal estate, in the event of the death of the other[33] (see chapter on General Principles for an explanation of Joint Tenant).

In the event of the remainder man (the one who gets the property on the passing away of a life tenant) killing the life tenant, the best course according to one school of thought would be to postpone the killer's enjoyment of the property until the time at which the life expectation of the tenant for life would terminate.

Finally it has been held[34] that the vendor under a contract for sale of land before conveyance takes place, is treated as a constructive trustee for the property the subject matter of the sale, until the actual transfer takes place.

[33] RE K (DECEASED) (1985) 1 ALL ER 403
[34] OUGHTRED v IRC (1960) AC 206; (1959) 3 W.L.R. 898; (1959) 3 ALL ER 623

CHAPTER 5

DISCRETIONARY &PROTECTIVE TRUSTS

WHAT ARE DISCRETIONARY TRUSTS AND WHAT ARE THE RIGHTS OF A BENEFICIARY?

Most of the rules applicable to discretionary trusts have been covered in the chapter relating to "CERTAINTY" e. g. the test for certainty of objects, the necessity for administrative workability, etc.

It must be emphasized that the beneficiary in a discretionary trust has no right to receive anything at all. He does, however, have a right to be _considered_ and a right to ensure due performance of the trust by way of action against the trust.

Collectively, the beneficiaries of a discretionary trust, if all are adult and under no disability, have the power to acquire the trust property by agreeing to put an end to the trust[35].

---

[35]   SAUNDERS v VAUTIER (1841) 10 LJ Ch 354

HOW THEN DOES A BENEFICIARY CONTROL THE TRUSTEE?

The most effective method by which the beneficiaries can control the powers of the trustees is by threatening to bring it to an end or actually bringing it to an end if they are in a position to do so. A 1928 case[36] confirmed that this can be done by beneficiaries of a discretionary trust.

An Individual Beneficiary under a Discretionary Trust does not hold a proprietary interest in a trust fund. In a 1968 case[37] a beneficiary under a discretionary trust died and the trustee successfully refused to pay death duty on his share on the grounds that he did not have a sufficient interest to be liable under it.

WHAT ARE PROTECTIVE TRUSTS?

Such a trust is employed when the settlor wishes to protect property against a reckless, negligent beneficiary and the possible resultant claims of his creditors. The main beneficiary is given a determinable life interest which is then followed by a discretionary trust for a class of beneficiaries of whom he may be one.

---

[36] RE SMITH (1928)
[37] RE GARTSIDE v IRC (1968) 2 W.L.R. 277; (1968) 1 ALL ER 121

THE DIFFERENCE BETWEEN A DETERMINABLE AND CONDITIONAL INTEREST

The difference is important as the court does not favour conditional interests and that is why protective trusts have to be devised in terms that make it <u>determinable and not conditional</u>.

A determinable interest is a limited interest, <u>its limit being set from the outset</u>.

A conditional interest is a full interest which is liable to be cut short by a condition that a particular event will occur subsequently (condition subsequent).

Words such as "while" "as long as" and "until" indicate a determinable interest and are valid.

Words such as "on condition that" and "provided that" indicate a conditional interest and courts do not favour this.

In a 1916 case[38], however, the settlor by settlement made before marriage gave property on trust to pay the income to himself for life or until certain events "should happen to me" of which one was bankruptcy. He went bankrupt and the trustee in

---

[38]   RE BURROUGHS v FOWLER (1916) Ch 251; 85 LJ CH 550

50

bankruptcy became entitled to his life interest. It did not stand as a protective trust.

A gift to a beneficiary until he becomes bankrupt is therefore valid unless he is attempting to guard against his own bankruptcy.

A settlor can protect himself against events other than bankruptcy.

In a 1889 case[39] there was a marriage settlement of the settler's own property until his bankruptcy or until he should suffer something whereby the same would, by operation of the law became payable to some other person and after such determination in trust to pay the income to his wife. A judgment creditor was appointed. Then the settlor was declared bankrupt. The wife was held entitled to the income because the determinable interest occured before he became bankrupt.

WHAT EVENTS GENERALLY GIVE RISE TO FORFEITURE OF ONES RIGHTS?

Decisions as to whether a determining event has occurred in a particular case must be read in the light of the definition of the determining event being considered.

---

[39]   RE DETMOLD (1889) 40 Ch D 585; 37 WR 442

In a 1943 case[40] the life tenant ceased to be entitled to receive the income of a trust because she lived in enemy territory during World War II. It became a discretionary trust in her favour as she went to live in enemy territory. This worked in her favour because the "Custodian of Enemy Property" in England could not then claim her interest. Therefore on forfeiture, the trust becomes a discretionary trust where the trustee can use his/her discretion as to when and how to pay the beneficiary forfeiture. The beneficiary has to _do_ an act to forfeit.

Forfeiture can be advantageous as a "Custodian of Enemy Property" cannot confiscate the property.

In a case[41] decided a year later the custodian was entitled to claim. The trust provided expressly that forfeiture was only to operate if the annuitant should "do or suffer any act" whereby the annuity should be payable elsewhere. Her failure to receive the annuity did not arise from her own act but merely from the rules governing residents in enemy territory. There was therefore no forfeiture and the custodian became custodian of the property.

---

[40]   RE GOURJUS WILL TRUST (1943) Ch 24; 59 TLR 47; (1942) 2 ALL ER 605
[41]   RE HALL (1944) Ch 46; 113 LJ Ch 76; (1943) 2 all er 753

CHAPTER 6

SECRET TRUSTS AND MUTUAL WILLS

HOW DOES ONE BENEFIT AN ILLEGITIMATE CHILD?

Once a person dies the executor who is the trustee applies to the court to have a will of the deceased probated. The will then becomes a public document. It can be inspected by anyone who pays the appropriate fee.

What if there was a testator of a will who wanted to secretly benefit his mistress or illegitimate child? The doctrine of secret trusts were developed to prevent the statutory provisions for the formal creation of trusts being used as an instrument fraud.

There are two types of secret trusts: Fully Secret Trusts and Half Secret Trusts.

FULLY SECRET TRUSTS

In a fully secret trust it appears from the will that the one named in the will takes the gift absolutely. What might have happened is that the person named in the will (X) would have previously agreed to the person making the will to hold it for another person (Y). For example a person Peter leaves his house in Diani to his friend John. This is what the will says. Actually what John would have done is to have previously agreed to Peter's request that he would hold it for Peter's illegitimate daughter Jane. In such a case John can be compelled to keep his commitment based on the fact that a secret trust was created. It is important that in secret trusts the obligation to hold the property in trust must have been accepted by the trustee before the death of the one who made the will.

A fully secret trust may be imposed on someone where the settler or testator during his or her lifetime communicated to the trustee terms of the trust and T accepted or acquiesced in the request.

The obligation imposed on T can even include a trust to leave property to a third party by way of a will. The above two principles were decided in a well-known case relating to certainty of subject matter[42].

---

42   OTTWAWAY v NORMAN (1972) Ch 698; (1972) 2 W.L.R. 50; (1971) 3 ALL E R 1325

WHAT ARE THE GROUNDS PREVENTING SECRET TRUSTS?

COURT OR CONSCIENCE?

If a testator did not wish to give any legal obligation in respect of the property, and only a moral duty. In a case decided in the 19th century[43], a testator made a will leaving his property to a Grogan. On his death bed he sent for Grogan and said that there was a letter with the will. But he did not ask Grogan to say that he would observe it. The letter named beneficiaries but also said "I do not wish you to act strictly to the foregoing instructions but leave it entirely in your good judgment to do as you think I would if living and as the parties are deserving" In fact Grogan gave nothing to one of the people named, who brought an action claiming that there was a secret trust in the letter, for the benefit of the person claiming.

It was held in that case that the testator had not intended a legally binding obligation and therefore there was no secret trust. To quote the court "The real question is what did he intend should be the sanction, was it the authority of a court of justice or the conscience of the devisee?"

---

[43]   MC CORMICK v GROGAN (1869) L R 4 H L 8 2; 1 7 W R 961

It was held to be exclusively the latter. The same principle was followed in a 1979 case[44].

EXISTENCE BUT NOT TERMS

Another ground preventing secret trusts are if the testator communicated the existence but not terms of the trust i.e. if the testator said there was a trust but did not say what it was about, it is not a valid trust and if someone accepted such a trust he or she would hold if for the beneficiaries of the testator. In a decided 19th century case[45], a testator had his will drawn up by a solicitor by which he left all his estate to the solicitor absolutely and appointed him executor in the same will. The testator told the solicitor prior to the drawing up of the will that he would communicate the terms of the trust by letter. No directions were given to the solicitor but after the testators death an unsigned document was found which was addressed to the solicitor instructing him to hold the whole estate for a Miss Brown.

The testator's next of kin went to court claiming that they were beneficiaries of the estate. The solicitor argued that there was a binding fully secret trust for someone else. The court held that there was no fully secret trust. The testator should

---

44   RE SNOWDEN (1979) Ch 528; (1979) 2 W.L.R. 654; (1979) 2 ALL E R 172

45   RE BOYES 26 Ch D 531; 32 WR 630

have communicated the terms of the trust during his lifetime. This he failed to do. This principle was followed in a 1937 case[46]. In that case by clause 5 of his will a testator gave £ 10,000 to his executors and trustees to be held on trust and disposed of by either of them during his lifetime. Before making his will the testator handed one of the executors a sealed envelope containing the name of the intended beneficiaries and directed her not to open the envelope until after the testators death. The trustee was not informed of the contents. It was held on appeal that as the sealed envelope was delivered before the date of the will it was not a communication consistent with the terms of the will and therefore there was no effective communication of the terms of the secret trust.

SILENCE

In another 19th century case[47] it was decided that a trust may be inferred from silence. A testator wished to apply his residuary estate to charity and was advised that he must give it absolutely to the legatees followed by a memorandum setting out how the residue might be divided amongst charities he wished to benefit. The testator left various properties equally to the three trustees A, B, & C. A copy of the terms of the trust and a copy

---

[46] RE KEEN (1937) Ch 236; 1937 1 ALL E R 452

[47] MOSS v COOPER (1861) 1 J & H 352; 4 L T 790

of the will was communicated to A, B & C and received by them. None of them made any express acceptance or refusal of the trust. The next of kin unsuccessfully challenged the disposition.

The communication and acceptance must therefore take place before the testator's death otherwise it is a ground preventing a secret trust. In a 19th century case[48] a testator bequeathed a legacy of £ 12,000 and certain properties to a Tebs and Martin (T&M) jointly. The testator contemplated devoting some of his property to charity and accordingly requested one of his executors to write a letter to T & M setting out the charitable objects he had in mind.

The executor wrote the letter and it was approved by the testator but it was not shown to T & M until after the testator's death. As neither T nor M had given an undertaking to the testator, it was held that since T & M knew nothing of the testator's intention until after his death they took the property absolutely.

WHAT IF THE "TRUSTEE" PREDECEASES THE SETTLOR OR WITNESSES HIS WILL

In a 1902 case[49] it was decided that if the proposed trustee predeceased the testator or is a

---

[48]   WALLGRAVE v TEBBS (1855) 2 K & J 313; 125 L J Ch 241

[49]   RE MADDOCK (1902) 2 Ch 270; 50 W R 598

58

witness to a will (which would make the bequest invalid) the property does not vest in the trustee and there is no secret trust. The property would then go to the residuary beneficiaries or it would be treated under the law as on intestacy (i.e. as though there was no will).

HOW DOES ONE PROVE IN A COURT OF LAW THAT A TRUST EXISTED?

According to 1979 case[50] if the claimant fails to establish evidence of the trust on a balance of probabilities (the kind of evidence a court requires in a civil case), then the claim fails. On the other hand if fraud is alleged the claimant has to prove this "beyond reasonable doubt" (the kind of stringent standard of proof that is required in a criminal court).

HALF SECRET TRUSTS

Half secret trusts arise in cases where on the face of the will property is given to A _as trustee_ but the terms of the trust do not appear in the will. Therefore indications are that there is a trust but the terms of the trust are secret. There is therefore no possibility for any fraud as is the case with a secret trust.

---

[50]   RE SNOWDEN (1979) Ch 528 (1979) 2 W.L.R. 654 (1979) 2 ALL E R 172

SPECIAL RULES AS TO HALF SECRET TRUSTS

The main issue however about half secret trusts in that communication and acceptance of the trust must be made before or at the same time of the making of the will instead of before the testator's death as is the case with fully secret trusts.
The terms of the trust must also be adequately communicated to the trustee.

DISTINCTIONS BETWEEN

FULLY SECRET TRUSTS	HALF SECRET TRUSTS
Communication and acceptance before testator dies.	Communication and acceptance at the same time as will.
There can be a contradiction in the will (i.e. trustee seems to take absolutely).	The trustee has to take as trustee.
Since trustee appears to take absolutely he cannot witness a will.	Since trustee takes as trustee he can witness a will.
If the trustee dies before the testator the trust fails.	If the trustee dies before the testator the trust does not fail.

There are decided cases to show that communication of the terms of a half secret trust must be done prior to the execution of a will.

COMMUNICATION AND "SILENCE"

In a case decided in 1929[51] a testator in his will left a legacy of £ 12,000 to 5 (five) persons upon trust "for the purpose indicated by me to them".

The testator informed one of the legatees in detail as to the objects of the trust and informed the other four in outline of the same before the execution of the will. The legacy was for his mistress and illegitimate son. The wife and child of the testator amongst others sought a declaration that it was not a valid trust because of the mere verbal communication of the trust.

It was held that a valid half secret trust was established for the mistress and illegitimate son because the purpose of the trust was communicated to the trustees and their resulting acquiescence.

Not only must communication of the terms of the trust be made prior to execution of the will but actual communication must be made in accordance with the terms of the will (e.g. time and method of communication). The same case decided that the will cannot contemplate communication of the terms of

---

51   BLACKWELL v BLACKWELL (1929) A-C 318; 98 L J Ch 251; 140 IT 444

the trust after execution of the will. The fact that communication of the terms of the trust must occur prior to the execution of the will was confirmed in a 1970 case[52]. It was decided in a 19th century case that if the trust property is land it must be evidenced in writing[53].

SOLICITOR LOSES BENEFIT OF THE DOUBT WHEN THERE IS A LAWYER-CLIENT RELATIONSHIP

It has been decided in a 1950 case[54] that if there is any doubt as to the amount that the trustee keeps as beneficiary, the trustee loses the benefit of the doubt in favour of the actual beneficiaries. In his will a testator appointed a friend and his solicitor to be executors trustees and bequeathed the whole of his property to his trustees "ABSOLUTELY, they, well knowing my wishes concerning the same". The testator told the trustees when making the will that he wished them to make certain payments out of the estate and retain the remainder for their own use. After the payments were made they claimed they were entitled to keep the surplus which was substantial. It was held that the trustees could not keep the surplus as a fiduciary obligation had been imposed on them.

---

52   RE BATEMANS WILL TRUSTS (1970) 1 W.L.R. 1463; (1970), 3 ALL E.R 817
53   RE BAILLIE (1886) 2 T L R 660
54   RE REES (1950) Ch 204; (1949), 2 ALL E R 1003

WHAT IF THERE IS NO DOUBT?

However, it was held in 1891[55] that the trustees may have a beneficial interest but only where there is convincing evidence that such was the testator's intention.

WHAT IF A TRUSTEE RECEIVES MORE TRUST PROPERTY THAN EXPECTED

If a trustee received under the will more property than he had agreed to hold, he holds it in trust for the residuary beneficiary.

This was held in a 1939 case[56], by his will a testator gave a £5000 legacy jointly to 2 persons to hold one secret trust which he had communicated to them before signing the will. He made another will increasing the amount by £5000 but did not communicate this increased amount before signing the codicil. It was held there was a secret trust of the first £5000 but not the second £5000.

---

[55]   RE TYLER (1891) 3 Ch 252; 60 L J Ch 686

[56]   RE COLLIN COOPER (1939) Ch 811 (1939) 3 ALL E R 586

MUTUAL WILLS

TRUST ONLY IMPOSED AFTER THE FIRST DEATH

Mutual Wills arise where two persons have an arrangement to make similar wills disposing of the property in a particular way. Usually a couple makes similar wills _in each other's favour_ and thereafter to the children. If there is an arrangement like this either party could withdraw from it _before the first death_. Once the first person, however, has died, the survivor holds the property on trust for the beneficiaries named in the will.

WHAT PROPERTY IS COVERED

The trust covers only property which the survivor receives from the estate of the first to die. It would sometimes also include the property the survivor owned at that time. The wills usually make the position clear, but there is no statutory provision to clarify this. In a 1981 case[57] an elderly couple had 3 children. They made wills in each other's favour absolutely and in default to their 3 children. In 1964 each of them reduced the share of 1 daughter to a life interest. After the husband's death, the wife made a new will

---

[57]   RE CLEAVER (1981) 2 ALL E R 1018; 1 W.L.R. 939

consistent with the original will and made two more wills, the last one leaving the entire estate to her daughter and her husband and nothing to her other 2 children.

It was held, on application to the court, that the executors held the estate on trust based on the 1964 will made when they were both alive. These wills were shown to be made simultaneously and in family conversations the wife having regarded herself as under an obligation to leave her estate to all her children confirmed this decision.

It was also held in this case that a survivor could enjoy in his or her life time the property but could not voluntarily dispose of it during his lifetime because of a fiduciary duty which crystallized upon the death of the first of the couple to pass away.

WHAT IF THE WILLS WERE IDENTICAL BUT WITH NO PROVISION AS TO IRREVOCABILITY?

In a 1925 case[58] a husband and wife made mutual wills in similar form, each spouse leaving his/her property to the other with the same provisions in the event if the other predeceasing. The wills were identical in terms. There was no

---

[58]   RE OLDHAM (1925) Ch 75; L J Ch 148; 132 L T 658

evidence, however, of any agreement that the wills should be irrevocable. After the husband's death the wife married again and made a new will which contradicted the earlier will.

It was held that the second will was upheld, the judge stating that even though the two wills were made in identical terms there was no evidence that the trust in the mutual will should be irrevocable by the survivor.

Therefore, all the following rules should apply in creating a trust in mutual wills:

(1) They should be in identical terms and simultaneously signed and dated.
(2) They should state that they are mutual wills.
(3) They should state that the mutual wills should be irrevocable by the survivor who took the benefit.
(4) The property under the trust should be specified e.g.

　　a) Only property which the survivor receives from the estate of the first to die.
　　b) It could include property the survivor owned at the time of death.
　　c) It could include property that either or both owned at the time of signing the wills.

CHAPTER 7

RESULTING TRUSTS

WHAT ARE RESULTING TRUSTS?

As the name possibly implies, the beneficial interest in a property results (or goes) back to the settlor (or his estates if he is deceased.) They are "automatic" resulting trusts. They are also called Implied Trusts as they arise from what would be deemed the intention of the settlor and not expressed by him or her.

In both cases, the trust arises in favour of the "transferor" of property in the absence of any actual evidence of an intention that he should be the beneficiary.

AUTOMATIC RESULTING TRUSTS

This might occur because the objects of the trusts are invalid or no beneficiary has been nominated. In a 1955 case[59], a trust was to be created "to A for life as she lives with B, remainder to B for life, remainder to the

---

[59]   RE COCHRANE (1955) Ch 309; (1955) 2 WLR 267

survivor." No beneficiary was properly nominated and so when A ceased to live with B there was a resulting trust for the settlor though both A and B were alive. In another case decided in 1974[60], a Mr. Vendervell directed his trustees to transfer shares to the Royal College of Surgeons to endow a Pharmacology "chair." The scheme was that £145,000 of dividends would be paid on the shares and an option to repurchase them would be exercised by the trustees for £5,000 giving the Royal College £150,000 in all. Because there was no beneficiary of the option there was a resulting trust in favour of Mr. Vendervell. The tax department successfully assessed Venderwell to Surtax on the dividends at £ 145,000 received by the Royal College.

Therefore because of a technicality, i.e. there was no beneficiary of the option Mr. Vandervell got a huge tax bill because the whole trust was deemed his.

An automatic resulting trust may also arise where property is given on trust for a specific purpose that only disposes a certain amount of property as is needed for the purpose and there will then be a resulting trust for the surplus[61] In the case in question fund of money was collected by

[60] VANDERVELL v IRC (1974)
[61] RE GILLINGHAM BUS DISASTER FUND (1959) Ch 62; (1958) 2 WLR 325; (1958) 2 ALL ER 749

subscription from the public to relieve the victims of a serious bus accident. Much of the money came from street collections and other sources which could never have been traced. A resulting trust was therefore imposed, with regard to the surplus, as no beneficiary could be found.

In a 1970[62] case a fund was set up to provide benefits for widows and dependants of the Police Force. The sources of funds were monthly subscriptions from members, proceeds of entertainment, raffles collection boxes and donations and legacies. On the ending of the fund because of the amalgamation of the force with another one, it was held that only legacies from known donors were returnable and therefore the surplus went to the crown as bona vacantia. (Goods or property without an apparent owner— going to the government).

PRESUMED RESULTING TRUSTS

In principle these arise where one party gets a greater share in the legal title to property than he has paid for, he is presumed to hold that "bonus" part on trust for the person who has, in effect, given it to him or her.

---

[62]   THE WEST SUSSEX CASE (1970) 2 WLR 848; 114 SJ 92

This can occur where

a) *A transfers a certain property to B, alone or jointly with A, B not having paid anything for it.*

b) *A, alone or with B, purchases property and the legal title to it is vested in B, alone or jointly with A, B having provided less than a proportionate share of the purchase price.*

B, in the above cases, is presumed to hold that part of the legal interest in the property which he has not paid for on resulting trust for A.

WHEN ARE "PRESUMED" RESULTING TRUSTS NOT PRESUMED?

1) *When A voluntarily conveys by way of conveyance, land to B.*

2) *A is the husband or father of B or stands in loco parentis (one who assumes liability for providing for a minor in the way a parent would do) to B.*

In a 1968[63] case A owned shares in a company and he registered them in the name of B by way of gift. B, however, orally disclaimed the gift. The company then wound up with a surplus of assets to be distributed to shareholders. The question for the court to decide was who owned the shares as

---

[63] RE PARADISE MOTOR CO. LTD (1968); 1 WLR 1125; (1968) 2 ALL ER 625, 1125 J 271

70

they both (A & B) claimed ownership of the shares. It was held that oral disclaimer by B caused a resulting trust to operate in favour of A.

The presumption of resulting trusts can be rebutted if evidence is produced that B was intended to benefit from the property. In an 1875[64] case A Mrs. Baker purchased stock in the joint names of herself and the son of her widowed daughter-in-law. As the son was a stranger (one not privy to or party to an act or transaction) in the circumstances he would have been regarded as holding the shares in resulting trust for the grandmother Mrs. Baker.

On an application being made in court on Mrs. Baker's death it was held that the evidence confirmed that a presumption of a resulting trust was rebutted and the son was entitled to the shares absolutely as that was the intention of Mrs. Baker.

On the other hand in a 1935[65] case, a woman transferred shares in the name of herself and her granddaughter who was only 4 years old. It was held that a resulting trust was held to accrue for the grandmother.

---

[64]   FOWKES v PASCOE (1875) LR 10 Ch APP 343; 44 LJ Ch 367
[65]   RE VINOGRADOFF (1935) WN 68

This case seemed unfair in the light of the previous case because why else would the grandmother transfer the property to joint names?

The general policy is that in the case of a voluntary transfer of property other than land i.e. personally, the weight of opinion favors a resulting trust i.e. it is more likely to be held on resulting trust if it involves assets other than land.

On the other hand, the presumption that it was a "presumed resulting trust" can be rebutted (presumption disproved) by evidence that a gift was not intended, unless the resulting evidence disclosed an illegal purpose as[66] where a husband purchased American Bonds and registered them in the name of the wife to avoid American Tax or[67] where the wife kept the assets he had built in the name of his wife to protect it from his creditors. In this case the wife again got to keep this windfall.

In a relatively recent case decided in 1987[68]. A lent £60,000 to a company run by a friend for the purpose of hiring equipment. The equipment was ordered and some money was spent on

---

[66] EMERYS INVESTMENT TRUSTS (1959) Ch 410; (1959) 2 W.L.R 461; (1959) 1 ALL ER 577
[67] GASCOIGNE v GASCOIGNE (1918) 1 KB 223; 34 TLR 168
[68] EVTR (1987)

temporary equipment. Before delivery of the bulk of the equipment the bankers decided to attach the assets of the company on it defaulting on a loan secured by a debenture. The bank claimed to be entitled to retain the balance of the money. A resisted and it was held by the courts that the purpose of the loan was to pay for the equipment and since the purpose failed, the money was held on a resulting trust for A, the lender. The bank could not claim this money, as there were resulting trusts on the failure of the purpose for which they were lent.

CHAPTER 8

CHARITABLE TRUSTS

WHAT ARE CHARITABLE TRUSTS?

WHAT ARE THE ESSENTIALS OF A CHARITY?

There is no legal definition of a charity. In a 1955[69] case it has been said that "there is no limit to the number and diversity of ways in which man will seek to benefit his fellow man".

The Charitable Uses Act 1601, set out in the preamble a test of charitable objects and is still used as a guide by the court.

Charities have traditionally been divided into four main heads;

1) Trusts for the relief of poverty.
2) Trusts for the advancement of religion.
3) Trusts for the advancement of education.
4) Other charitable purposes.

To decide whether any particular purpose is charitable, it is necessary to decide, first, whether

---

[69] IRC v BADDELEY (HL 1955)

74

the purpose is beneficial i.e. that the act is of a "charitable nature", and secondly, whether the purpose is sufficiently public so as to distinguish it from private trusts.

The benefit must be assessed in the light of current circumstances so that what was once held to be beneficial might cease to be so, and vice versa, according to changing social needs and values.

TRUSTS FOR THE RELIEF OF POVERTY

In a 1951 case[70] it was said "poverty does not mean destitution, it is a wide and somewhat indefinite import (meaning); it may not be unfairly paraphrased for present purposes as meaning persons who have to go short in the ordinary acceptance of that term, due regard to their status in life and so forth.

If there are persons within the class of beneficiaries who are not poor, the Trust will not qualify. In a 1930 case[71], the testator left money for a trust to provide clothing for boys between certain ages, sons of parents resident in FARNHAM. Nobody who was supported by a charitable institution or whose parents were on

---

[70]   RE COULTHURST (1951) Ch 661; 95 SJ 188
[71]   RE GWYON (1930) 1 Ch 255; 99 LJ Ch 104

Parish relief should be eligible. It was held that the provision was not for the relief of poverty as some boys were specifically excluded and rich boys were not excluded.

There is no objection that the recipient must pay something for the benefit of hospital services.

In a 1969 case[72], a testator died in 1963 leaving a large bequest "to the Sisters of Charity for 200 years or for so long they shall conduct St Vincent's private hospital, whichever shall be the shorter period, to be applied for the general purposes for such hospital".

This was held to be a valid charitable bequest for the relief of the sick even though payment was received.

In a 1983 case[73], a housing association, an incorporated charity, whose objects included inter-alia provision of housing for elderly persons in need of such accommodation, wished to build self-contained houses for elderly persons, on long lease in consideration of a capital sum. The charity commissioners doubted that it was charitable. It was held that the schemes were charitable being relief of the aged.

72   RE RESCH'S WILL TRUST (1969) 1 AC 514; (1968) 3 WLR 1153
73   ROWNTREE HOUSING ASN v AG (1983) Ch 159; (1983) 2 WLR 284

76

It is no objection that the class of beneficiaries is small in number or related or employed by the settlor.

In a 1972 case[74], a testator directed the trustees of his will to invest £10,000 and apply the income thereof in paying pensions to poor employees of Dingle Co. At the death of the testator the company had 705 full time and 189 part time employees and was paying pension to 89 employees.

It was held to be a valid trust as it relieved poverty amongst a particular description of poor persons and not named persons. The latter would have been a private trust.

EDUCATIONAL TRUSTS

The concept of education in this context is broad and includes both teaching and research in scholarly, practical or cultural matters.

In a 1957 case[75], George Bernard Shaw left a bequest to inquire into the value of an improved phonetic alphabet to show the waste of time and labor in using the current alphabet. It was held to be non-charitable as it merely increased knowledge without providing for the

---

[74]   DINGLE v TURNER (1972) AC 601; (1972) 2 WLR 523; (1972) 1 ALL ER 878
[75]   RE SHAW (1957) 1 WLR 729; (1957) 1 ALL ER 745

dissemination of that knowledge by teaching and education.

In 1923[76], a testator left a sum of money in trust for the Spiritualist Alliance for the establishment of a college for the training of mediums (persons who act as spiritual mediums exercising the power of telepathy or clairvoyance). This was held not to be a valid charity.

In 1965[77], a testator left his studio and its contents comprising pictures, antique furniture and some silver, china, and miniatures to be offered to the National Trust to be kept as a studio and maintained as a collection. The National Trust declined the offer and the executors of the estate applied to the court for directions. Expert evidence showed that the studio was squalid and contained little of worth and of no educational value for the public and so it was held in the court of appeal that it was not a charitable gift for the advancement of education.

A testator in a 1957 case[78] to left an estate "for the advancement and propagation of the teaching of socialized medicine, towards the furtherance of knowledge of socialist application of medicine to

[76]   RE HUMMULTENBERG (1923) 1 Ch 237; 92 LJ Ch 326
[77]   RE PINION (1965) Ch 85; (1964) 2 WLR 919; (1964) 1 ALL ER 890
[78]   RE BUSHNELL (1975) 1 WLR 1596;

public and personal health . . . . (which) can only be enjoyed in a socialist state." The trust was held to be political and therefore not charitable.

In a 1982 case[79], Amnesty International, an incorporated non-profit body was set up to ensure prisoners of conscience throughout the world were treated according to the UN Declaration on Human Rights. After the charity commissioners once refused to grant it Charitable Status an application was made to the court for a declaration as to its status. It was held to be not charitable as the purpose was found to be political.

In a 1972 case[80], The Incorporated Council of law reporting was set up for the preparation and publication in a convenient form, at a moderate price and under gratuitous professional control, of reports of judicial decisions of the English courts. It was a non-profit making body, whose reports were used by judges and the legal profession as well as law students. It was declared a charity in the court of appeal. It was not for political purposes.

One could not have a trust for members of particular families. In a 1945 case[81] it was held to be non-charitable where a trust was set up for the

---

[79]   MC GOVERN v AG (1982) Ch 321; (1982) WLR 222
[80]   INCORPORATED COUNCIL OF LAW REPORTING VG (1972) Ch 73; (1971) 3 WLR 853; (1971) 3 ALL ER
       1029
[81]   RE COMPTON (1945) Ch 123; 114 LJ Ch 99

benefit of three named families. It was also held to exclude trusts for the children of employees of a particular company.

RELIGIOUS TRUSTS

The public benefit requirement for religious trusts is formulated in a similar way to Educational Trusts but it is very easily arrived at.

It is said that the courts assume that the public derives an indirect benefit from the religious beliefs of even a small number of adherents[82].

In 1962[83] it was decided that a trust for the saying of masses can be charitable if it can satisfy the public benefit for charitable trusts.

On the other hand where believers are secluded from the rest of the society and no other public benefit can be proved, that religious trust will fail to be charitable.

In a 1949 case[84] masses which were said in a private chapel to which the public were not admitted and were said for the souls of deceased persons were said to lack the public benefit and therefore not charitable.

---

[82] OPPENHEIM v TOBACCO SECURITIES TRUST (1951) AC 297; (1951) 1 ALL ER 31

[83] RE WATSON (1973); 1 WLR 1472 (1973) 3 ALL ER 678

[84] NEVILLE ESTATES vs MADDEN (1962) Ch 832; (1961) 3 WLR 999

In a 1989 case[85], the testatrix, a devout Roman Catholic and regular worshipper at church, included in her will gifts as follows;

"I wish to leave £2000 to the Roman Catholic Church Bishop for masses for the repose of the souls of my husband and parents and my sisters when I die. Whatever is left over my estate is to be given to the Roman Catholic Church for masses of my soul." It was held that the trust, for a religious purpose contained the necessary element of public benefit and therefore was charitable. This was held (in view of the edifying and imposing effect of the celebration of a religious service) to be a sufficient public benefit.

TRUSTS FOR SPORTS OR RECREATION

Sports itself is not a charitable purpose but sporting facilities provided as an ancillary to some other charitable purpose which enhances that purpose will be charitable.

In a 1981 case[86], a football association set up a trust, the objects being the furtherance of education of schools and universities to ensure due attention given to the physical education

---

[85] GILMOUR v COATS (1949) 1 A.C. 426; (1949) LJR 1034
[86] HETHERINGTON, GIBBS v MCDONNEL (1989)

and character development of pupils at such schools or universities. This was held to be a trust.

In a 1953 case[87] a police association provided recreational activities and facilities for the police. It was held it promoted efficiency of the police force and preservation of public order and therefore charitable.

It has been also held[88] that it is charitable to provide parks and similar places for outdoor recreation by the general public in a particular location.

CONCLUSION

Trusts which are for purposes beneficial to the community will be enforceable if they are considered to be charitable.

A number of rules affecting the validity of a private trust are relaxed in the case of trusts for exclusively charitable objects:

If the intention is absolute but the object is uncertain or the object become illegal, the charitable intention will be effected.

[87] IRC vs MC MULLEN (1981) AC 1 (1980); 2 WLR 416
[88] IRC v CITY IF GLASGOW POLICE ATHLETIC ASN (1953) AC 380; (1953) 2 WLR 625; (1953) 1 ALL ER 747

The rule against perpetual duration do not apply.

The rules against remoteness of vesting does not apply to a gift over from one charity to another. Therefore a transfer from one charity to another can take place long after the time limit for vesting of property.

WHERE TREATMENT IS SAME AS FOR PRIVATE TRUSTS.

Separation of lawful and unlawful objects possible, the latter being invalid.

When capital vests, (gives a present right to the immediate possession of property) directions to accumulate income are invalid.

The trust must have a trustee.

WHAT ARE THE REQUISITES OF A VALID CHARITABLE TRUST?

The donor must have the capacity to deal with the estate and must have a disposable estate.

The mode of donation must not be illegal.

The application of the charity must be a legal obligation and exclusively charitable.

The amount of the gift must be ascertained.

CY-PRES—WHAT IS THE CY-PRES DOCTRINE?

If a non-charitable trust is initially ineffective or subsequently fails it generally goes back to the settlor as a resulting trust. In the case of a charitable trust, the trust property can be applied for another charitable purpose as close as possible to the original trust. This is the cy-pres doctrine. For the doctrine to apply two conditions must be fulfilled. The original purpose must be impossible or impractical and secondly the donor must have shown a paramount intention to benefit charity.

Cy-Pres also applies;

Where only part of the property is possible to use according to a specified charitable purpose

Where such property can be more effectively used in another way when taking into account the spirit of the gift.

The original purpose is adequately provided for by other means.

Where the purpose ceases to be a suitable method of using property.

CHAPTER 9

APPOINTMENT, RETIREMENT & REMOVAL OF TRUSTEES

Statute law limits the number of trustees to a maximum number (save for charitable trusts).

APPOINTMENT OF TRUSTEES

Initial Trustees

The first trustees are generally appointed in the will or settlement. If a settlor fails to appoint trustees or if they predecease him, the property will be held by the personal representatives of the settlor. In both cases the property will be held on the terms of the trust or settlement.

Where one of the initial trustee dies the property vests in the survivor (s). When the last survivor dies, the property vests in his / her personal representatives, again subject to the trust.

APPOINTMENT OF SUBSEQUENT TRUSTEES

The settlor cannot appoint new trustees once the trust has been properly constituted, unless there is an express power for him to do so. Although beneficiaries can terminate a trust they cannot appoint a new one.

Statutory power

Unless there is a contrary provision in the trust instrument Statute Law provides that a replacement trustee may be appointed where:

a) The trustee is dead (including a person appointed in a will who dies before the testator).
b) The trustee remains outside the country for a continuous period exceeding 12 months
c) The trustee wants to retire.
d) The trustee refuses to act or disclaims before accepting office.
e) The trustee is unfit to act as when he is bankrupt.
f) The trustee is incapable of acting.
g) The trustee of an implied, resulting or constructive trust is an infant.
h) The trustee is removed under a power in the trust instrument.

Statute Law allows for additional trustees to be appointed in any case where there are not more than a certain number of trustees.

An appointment must be made in writing and should be made by:

86

a) The persons nominated in the trust instrument for the purpose of appointing new trustees or failing such a person;
b) The surviving or continuing trustees.
c) The personal representatives of the last surviving or continuing trustee.
d) The court.

Where a trustee is being replaced, anyone can be appointed a new trustee including the appointer himself.

Appointment by the court

The court has a wide power to appoint new trustees "either in substitution for or in addition to any existing trustee or trustees or although there is no existing trustee/s". In particular the court may appoint a new trustee where an existing trustee is mentally unfit to act or is a bankrupt, or being a corporation, is in liquidation or has been dissolved. The court will not appoint a person excluded from being a trustee under section 37 (i.e. a person under a mental disability or living abroad).

VESTING OF TRUST PROPERTY

The trust property has to be vested in the new trustees. Where the trustee is appointed by deed a vesting declaration in the deed will vest the property in the trustees and such declaration may be implied subject to any provision in the deed to the contrary. There is no need for an express conveyance or assignment.

a) Land mortgaged to secure money subject to a trust.
b) Land held under a lease which contains a covenant against assignment (an agreement creating an obligation in a deed not to assign) without consent unless the consent has been obtained before the execution (signing, sealing and delivery in the presence of witnesses) of the deed.
c) Stocks and shares.

Exception (a) keeps the trust off the title. Trustees who lend money on mortgage do not disclose the existence of the trust. On the appointment of a new trustee there must be a separate transfer of the mortgage. The borrower will thus know whom to repay the money without inspecting the trust instrument and deeds of appointment.

Exception (b) prevents the appointment causing a breach of covenant against assigning even if inadvertent.

Exception (c) recognises that legal title to shares can only be effected by registration with the relevant company.

ENDING OF TRUSTEESHIP

1. BY DISCLAIMER

When disclaiming a trust it is advisable, though not essential, to do so by deed. If the trustee disclaiming is the sole trustee the trust property will revert to the settlor or his personal representatives upon trust.

2. BY RETIREMENT

A trustee may retire by deed from the trust provided that either a trust corporation or two trustees will be left after his retirement and his co-trustees and the person, if any, entitled to appoint new trustees consent by deed. Mortgages, leases with a covenant against assignment (an agreement creating an obligation in a deed not to assign) and stocks and shares will have to be transferred separately on appointment.

3. BY REPLACEMENT

A trustee may retire on being replaced by someone else.

4. BY REMOVAL

The court has the power to vest trust property in new trustees and to remove a trustee. In exercising the power to appoint new trustees, the continuing trustees should have regard to the best interests of the trust. The wishes of the beneficiaries although relevant are not determinative unless they are prepared to put an end to the trust. This was confirmed in a case[89] where a testator directed that his small residential estate should be held in trust for his wife for life with remainder to his children. Two trustees were appointed by will to administer the trusts. One of the trustees wished to retire. He and the beneficiaries wished to appoint LIoyds Bank in his place. The other trustees refused to join in on this as it was too expensive for such a small estate. The beneficiaries took out a summons asking the court to order the trustees to concur with them.

It was held that the beneficiaries were not entitled to control the direction of the trustees in this way, nor would the court interfere. The trustees were therefore entitled not to appoint a bank for this small estate.

It was decided in an 1866 case[90], that where the court is asked to appoint trustees, it will follow the following principles:

[89]   RE: BROCKBANK (1948) CH 206; (1948) LJR 952; (1948) 1 ALL ER 287
[90]   RE: TEMPEST (1866) L.R. 1 CH APP. 485; 35 LJ CH 622

1) The court will have regard to the wishes of persons by whom the trust is created.
2) The court will not appoint a person with interests in opposition to the testator or other beneficiaries. It has a duty to hold an even hand.
3) The court will have regard as to whether the appointment will promote or impede execution of the trust and therefore will not appoint a minor or a person living abroad.

In an 1884 case[91] it was decided that the court has an inherent jurisdiction to remove a trustee and appoint a new one in his place or even remove him without appointing a replacement. In this case a board of executors of Cape Town were the sole surviving executors and trustees of the will of a Jacob Letterstedt. A beneficiary alleged misconduct on their part in the administration of the trust and claimed that the board was unfit to act and should be removed. Although the allegations were not substantiated by the beneficiaries all trust and respect between the trustees and beneficiaries were broken down. The court removed the trustees.

---

[91]   LETTERSTEDT v BROERS (1884) 9 APP Cas. 371; 53 L.J. PC 44

CHAPTER 10

POWERS OF TRUSTEES

This chapter deals with powers of maintenance, advancement and delegation of Trustees.

Maintenance

a) Before the beneficiary reaches 18 the trustees may pay to his parent or guardian or otherwise apply, the whole or part of the income of the property for his maintenance, benefit or education.
b) After 18 if the beneficiary has still not got a vested interest, then the trustees must pay the whole of the income to the beneficiary.

In both the above cases there must not be any indication of a contrary intention in the trust instrument or deed.

All the income arising during infancy which is not distributed should be accumulated and invested. If necessary the trustees can apply the accumulation for the benefit of any infant beneficiary as if they were income from the current year.

The beneficiary is entitled to accumulation of income on reaching his majority (or earlier marriage) if either he is then entitled to the capital or during his minority he had a vested interest in the income.

The court has a statutory power to sell a minors property to provide funds for his maintenance.

Generally contingent (that which awaits or depends on the happening of an event) gifts generally carry the intermediate income but it was decided in a 1963 case[92] that a residuary bequest which is contingent and postponed to a future date does not carry the intermediate income.

In this case the testator devised certain land to his daughter, the gift not to take effect until after the wife's death. The 21 year old daughter failed to be entitled to income while the wife lived.

A beneficiary under a discretionary trust does not have an interest in the trust.[93]

One should however, note the possibility of the court using its inherent jurisdiction to authorise

---

[92]   RE MC GEORGE (1983); Ch 544 1992 W.L.R. 767; (1963) 1 ALL E.R. 51

[93]   RE VESTEYS SETTLEMENT (1951) Ch 209; 2 ALL ER 891 (1950) 2 ALL ER 891

maintenance out of capital where there is no other means of the infant's support.[94]

Advancement

Unless there is a contrary intention in the trust instrument or deed all trustees have a statutory power to pay capital for the advancement or benefit of any person entitled to the capital or any share thereof even if there is a possibility that the beneficiaries interest may be defeated.

Besides being limited to personal property there are limitations of the statutory power of advancement. The capital advanced must not exceed half the beneficiary's vested (right to possession) or presumptive (conclusive evidence as to a share). 34 (1) (iii) the advance must not prejudice the prior life, or other interest of any person (e. g. life tenant) unless he has given his written consent.

The court has the power to order that an infant's property be transferred so that the capital or income can be applied for the maintenance, education or benefit of the infant.

Two principles resulted from a 1964 case[95]:

94   WELLESLEY v WELLESLEY (1828) 2 Bli (NS) 124
95   PILKINGTON v IRC (1964) AC 612; (1962) 3 W.L.R. 1051; (1962) 3 ALL ER 622

94

1. *The trustees are restricted to applying or paying money for the advancement or benefit of the beneficiary under the trust. These words have been construed to mean "setting up the beneficiary in life" as opposed to "making mere casual payments to him". It covers purchasing a business premises, a settlement on marriage, providing the means to enter an apprenticeship or supplying further capital to an existing business.*

2. *Advancement or benefit includes an advance to resettle on a new tax efficient trust*

In another 1964 case[96], the following principles were established:

1. *The power of advancement can only be exercised if it is for the benefit of the child to have a share of the capital before his or her time. It should only be used where there is some good reason for it and not with some other benefit in view.*

2. *If a bank pays a child it could not properly leave the child entirely free, legally and morally to spend it in any way with responsibility on their part to enquire as to its application.*

---

[96]   RE PAULINGS SETTLEMENT TRUSTS (1964) Ch 303; (1963) 3 W.L.R. 742; (1963) 3 ALL ER 1

3. Where money is advanced for a particular purpose the child advanced is under a duty to apply it for that purpose.
4. Where a trustee carries out a transaction in breach of trust with the apparent consent of the beneficiaries he would still be liable if he knew the child was under undue influence (where a person deals with property etc., when he has not been allowed to exercise a free and deliberate judgement in the matter) of someone like the child's parent.
5. Undue influence can be presumed to have taken place and continued for a short time after the child attains adulthood.

This case concerned money under a settlement for four children squandered by the family. An action was brought by the four children against the Trustee Bank. The bank was liable for all but 2 advances.

Delegation

"Trustees or personal representatives may, instead of acting personally, employ and pay an agent whether an advocate, banker, stockbroker or other person to transact any business or do any act required to be transacted or done in the execution of the trust, or the administration of the testators or intestates estate including the receipt and payment of money and shall be

96

entitled to be allowed and paid all charges and expenses so incurred and shall not be responsible for the default of any such agent if employed in good faith". [needs reference]

The law was that a trustee could not delegate his trust powers as he was selected for his knowledge and personal qualities. Trustees have, however, always been able to delegate where special skills are required (e. g. stock broker or advocate).

The effect of this section is that trustees no longer have to show a special need for expertise before they can delegate.

Statute Law:

a. exempts the trustee from vicarious liability (liability which falls on one person as the result of an action by another) for the action of agents. This, however, does not exempt a trustee from liability for failing to supervise.
b. gives trustees wide powers to delegate where the trust property is outside country.
c. provides that trustees may appoint advocates and bankers to receive trust moneys, but the trustees will be liable if they permit the property to remain in control of the advocate or banker for longer than necessary.

In a 1931 case[97], it was held that where an agent is appointed under S 24 (1) it appears that the trustee is not liable for the agents default so long as the trustee acted in good faith at all relevant times. In that case a sole executor appointed a solicitor to wind up the estate and at that time the executor had no reason to doubt the suitability of the solicitor. On the solicitor absconding it was held that the executor was not liable as there was no wilful default on the part of the executor/trustee.

In a 1883 case[98], it was held that the trustee may be liable for his own default either in failing to choose an agent or failing to supervise him properly. In this case a trustee employed a stock broker to invest £5000 in trust funds. The broker misappropriated the funds and the beneficiaries sued the trustee for breach of trust. The trustee was held not liable as he had acted prudently on appointing the broker.

The trustee would, however be expected to exercise proper care in choosing his agent and to employ him in his proper line of business or profession.

---

[97] RE VICKERY (1931) Ch 572; 100 LJ Ch 138
[98] SPEIGHT v GAUNT (1883) 9 App. Cas 1 32 WR 435

In a 1968 case[99], trustees who owned 70% of the company were held liable when a manager misappropriated company funds; they failed to supervise a manager appointed by the company in which the trust had a majority shareholding.

The court considered various methods by which a trustee who has a controlling interest could place himself in a position to make informed decisions as to how to protect the assets:

1. *By running the business himself as Managing Director (MD)*
2. *By becoming an NED (Non-Executive Director) (a director who only sits inboard meetings and not involved in the management) and having the business managed by someone else.*
3. *By appointing a nominee to the board to report to him from time to time.*
4. *Receipt of BOD (Board of Directors) minutes, monthly management accounts or quarterly reports.*

---

[99]   LUCKINGS WILL TRUSTS (1968) 1 W.L.R. 866; 3 1967 ALL E.R. 726

CHAPTER 11

INVESTMENT DUTIES OF TRUSTEES

While the law sets out what authorized investments a trustee is allowed to invest in, a trustee who complies with the statute will not necessarily be immune from attack by beneficiaries.

Even an authorized investment in certain circumstances can result in a breach of the trustees general duties of care and impartiality.

The duty of the trustee when investing trust funds would be to take such care as an ordinary prudent man would take as if he were under a duty to beneficiaries to whom he felt morally bound.

He should also ensure a proper balance between reasonable income and preservation of the capital to those entitled to it in remainder (situation where A grants land to B for life and thereafter to C and his heirs—C's interest is a remainder). In a nutshell if income is earned it should not be so high as to deplete the capital.

He must also ensure that there is a proper diversification of investments. Trustee can only invest in authorized investments. Authorized investments are:

1. Those investments which are authorized by the will or trust deed; and
2. Those authorized by statute.

A Trustee may invest any trust fund in his hands whether in a state of investment or not. He can invest:

1. In any securities in which trustees are for the time being authorized to invest in.
2. In any securities the interest on which is for the time being guaranteed by any public debentures issued under the authority of and guaranteed by any act.
3. Any security issued by a municipal authority under the Local Government Act and which the minister has gazetted that it is a trustee security under this act.
4. Company listed in a recognized Stock Exchange and who has paid up share capital is over a certain amount and has been paying dividends for the previous 5 years. This includes any successor to this company as gazetted by the Registrar of Companies.
5. In any mutual funds.
6. Any shares of a building society.

7. Any immovable property either in fee simple (absolute ownership clear of any condition, limitation or restriction) or for a government lease exceeding 40 years and where the land rent does not exceed 4% and it does not include a re-entry provision apart from default on rent or mortgage payments.

Statute authorized investments can be divided into 2 broad divisions:

a. Fixed interest investments.
b. Wider range investments.

Fixed interest securities are:

a. A security which under its terms of issue, bears a fixed rate of interest.
b. A mortgage of immovable property or other financial institution.

An investment which bears a fixed rate of interest or a mortgage of immovable property or a deposit in a savings institution.

Wider range securities are defined in the Act. A wider range security means a security other than a fixed interest security. Fixed interest securities have minimal risk and steady returns whereas wider range securities have higher returns and higher but acceptable risks.

When a trustee decides to invest he must divide the trust funds into:

a. The fixed interest part and
b. The wider range part.

He must do this if he wishes to invest in wider range security. If the trustee decides to invest on wider range securities, 50 % of the funds must be in a fixed interest security. The trust fund is therefore split in half, one portion or more on fixed interest securities and the balance in wider range securities.

He can of course invest all the funds in fixed interest securities. Because the statutory powers are considered to be inadequate, by many professional advisers and in effect by the court, it is common for trust deeds to contain very wide powers of investment.

In a 1983 case[100], inflation was considered to be a "special circumstance" enabling the grant of wider powers of investment to a co-operative society pension fund.

In a 1984 case[101], it was held that the court should be ready to grant an extension of powers

[100]   MASON vs FARBROTHER (1983) 2 ALLER 1078
[101]   TRUSTEES OF THE BRITISH MUSEUM v AG (1984) 1 W.L.R. 418 (1984) 1 ALLER 337

in suitable cases, judging by each case on its merits.

The word "invest" is frequently used in trust instruments and in the following two cases, the question has arisen of whether an investment clause so worded permitted the purchase of assets which yield capital gains rather than income.

In a 1919 case[102], a testator left his estate on trust for his children in equal shares. The trustees were given power to invest in any stocks, funds, shares and security or other investments as they in their absolute discretion thought fit. They were to have the same power of investing as if they were absolutely and beneficially entitled to the property.

The trustees asked the court if they had the power to invest in real property. It was held that since the word "invest" had as one of its meanings to apply money in the purchase of some property from which interest or profit is expected, the power given to the trustees permitted them to purchase real estate if it was bought as an investment.

In a 1947 case[103], the trust investment contained an investment clause which required all money

---

[102]   RE WRAGG (1919) 2 Ch 58; 88 LJ Ch 269
[103]   RE POWER (1947) Ch 572; (1947) 2 ALLER 282

104

to be invested by the trustee in any manner which he may, in his absolute discretion, think fit in all respects as if he were the sole beneficial owner of such money, including the purchase of freehold properties in the UK.

The trustee asked the court if this permitted him to purchase a house with vacant possession for the rent free occupation of the beneficiary.

It was held that the clause did not permit this because the word "Investment" connoted yield of income. It did not authorize the purchase of a house for rent free occupation as that would not produce an income.

In a 1887 case[104], trustees invested £3000 on the security of a mortgage, in a brick-field following competent advice given to them by a firm of valuers. The valuer's report was based on the assumption that the brick-field remained a going concern but went on to emphasize that it was nearly worked out. The trustees ignored this warning and the investment failed. The trustees were sued "as they had not acted with ordinary prudence but had made a hazardous investment" according to the plaintiffs. It was held that they must avoid investments which

104 LEAROYD vs WHITELY (1887) 12 APP CAS 727; 36 WR 721

are of a speculative or hazardous character. They must always consider whether the proposed investment is one which is prudent and correct for them as trustees and not businessmen to make.

In 1985 it was held[105] that the trustee should avoid speculative investments but otherwise attempt to choose investments which would be most rewarding to the beneficiaries regardless of the trustees own personal interests or social and political views.

In an even more recent case in 1987[106] paid trustees sought the courts approval for a draft scheme to extend their powers of investment to acquisition of any property as if they were beneficial owner of the investment fund. It was noted that the AG had no objections. It was held that "having regard to the size of the fund, the eminence of the trustees, the provisions of the scheme for obtaining and acting on advice and the quality of advice available etc. it was not necessary to require that part of the fund should be invested in fixed interest investments.

---

[105] COWAN vs SCARGILL (1984) 3 W.L.R. 501; (1984) 2 ALLER 750
[106] STEEL vs WELLCOME TRUSTEES (1988)

CHAPTER 12

TRUST CORPORATIONS

WHAT IS A TRUST CORPORATION?

This has been defined as a company which is empowered by its Memorandum of Association (constitution) "to undertake trusts" (provided that the said company shall not by any document issued by it or on its behalf hold out (or represent) that any liability attaches the Public Trustee (or consolidated fund) in respect of any act or omission of that body corporate when acting as an executor or administrator." Therefore that company cannot blame the Public Trustee for any of its acts or omissions.

WHAT SERVICES CAN A TRUST CORPORATION THEREFORE OFFER?

Executor and Trustee Services

Where a will appoints an executor (who acts as trustee) he ensures that the provisions of the will are followed exactly.

Such persons are usually family members, a lawyer or a trust corporation. If a family member is appointed such person usually appoints an advocate or a trust corporation to undertake the effective distribution for a fee. As trustee an advocate or trust corporation is under a duty to act in utmost good faith to carry out the wishes of the testator.

The trust corporation can also act as administrator of an estate where there is no will or when the administrator is unable or does not wish to act. In such cases the court usually appoints it.

In some cases the trust corporation is appointed joint executor or trustee with a family member, by the one creating the trust.

A trust corporation will undertake the responsibility of administering the estate if an individual and its specialist staff are readily accessible so that problems can be discussed without delay and in complete confidence, The company is able to exercise absolute impartially and is always available to act when required to do so.

While trust law requires the trust corporation to act completely impartially and in good faith, the employees of the trust corporation who deal as trustees are usually or should be obliged to be university graduates and/or professionals and have in their employment contracts clauses requiring confidentiality.

Family Trusts

A family trust is a legally binding arrangement between the person who introduces assets into the trust (the settlor) and reliable persons (trustees) — i.e. a trust corporation. They hold and administer the assets for the benefit of the beneficiaries and in accordance with the terms of the trust deed.

Trusts provide a highly confidential and flexible means of holding assets or conducting business. Also, assets held in trust for a beneficiary prevents the need and expense for assets to be transmitted on the death of the settlor (or testator). (This usually requires court applications).

Portfolio Investments

Many people have a portfolio of stock exchange investments. Others have spare cash to invest in the stock exchange but do not have the time or expertise to invest in or to manage their portfolio.

Investments in stocks and shares need regular and serious attention.

The trust corporation can give the necessary attention to such matters. They would have qualified people to analyze company balance sheets and prospectuses.

Property Management

Trust Corporation often also gets involved in the management of commercial and residential property for property owners. Such people do not have the time or energy to deal with matters relating to tenancy e. g. rent collection, maintenance, repairs etc.

Debentures

A trust corporation can act as trustee for the holders of debentures and unsecured loan stock. This would involve the preparation and signing of trusts deeds or trust indenture.

Corporate Trustee

Often public companies which are listed on a stock exchange have hundreds or even thousands of shareholders. They need corporate trustees not only to handle the share transfers but also deal with inquiries from shareholders. They are often called "Registrars".

They also act as trustees for the issue of bonus shares, rights issues, consolidation of shares, take-overs and mergers.

This requires specialized and experienced staff especially with computerization of records that take place now. A trust corporation is ideally placed for this.

Often trust companies act as "escrow" agents holding on to documents (or even share transfers) as escrow agent (trustee) until certain conditions are fulfilled. Such roles can adequately be undertaken by trust companies as corporate trustee.

Charitable and Educational Trusts

Trust corporations are well placed to administer charitable and educational trusts because of the permanent nature of such trusts. Such trusts have a trust deed and the trust company is usually best placed to administer such trusts. (Expertise, continuity, and impartiality).

Mortgage Brokerage

Sometimes individuals require loans and they need to be put in touch with a lending institution and the appropriate contracts are made. Conversely there are persons who have large sums of money who wish to lend their money out with (or without) security. They need to get in touch with reliable borrowers and the appropriate documentation prepared and signed by both parties. Mortgage brokers are able to put such people in touch with each other, for a fee. A trust corporation is well placed for this kind of service.

WHAT ARE THE ADVANTAGES OF APPOINTING A TRUST COMPANY TO UNDERTAKE SUCH SERVICES?

Continuity and Stability

A trust company has perpetual existence and are bound by trust laws. The chances of a trust company acting reliably as trustee are far better therefore than a private individual.

Reputation and Professionalism

A trust corporate will have the reputation and professionalism that a private individual usually will not have. They will be competent persons dealing with their clients and the trust company will have had a reputation for competent service.

Why not a lawyer?

Generally a lawyer does have the professionalism. He or she also is bound by trust laws.

On the other hand a lawyer-client relationship is a personal one and such relationships last as long as the lawyer is alive. What happens if such a lawyer passes away? Will the firm continue? This is usually the case if the lawyer will have sold his practice or had partners. Then it is a whole new ball game. A trust company usually has continuity and stability.

Affiliation with offshore trust corporation

Certain countries like the Channel Islands in the UK, Bahamas and now Mauritius are tax free zones. Such areas have trust entities which can serve a useful means of protection of assets and accumulation of tax free funds that cannot be confiscated by Governments and that have the added advantage of avoidance of probate, death, duty etc.

Trust companies affiliated to such offshore trust companies provide an added service to clients.

CHAPTER 13

SAMPLE REVOCABLE TRUST

Known as

_____

Dated: _____

PREAMBLE

Agreement made and executed this _____ day of _____, 20____, by and between hereinafter, referred to as the Grantor, and as the Trustee.

WHEREAS

Grantor desires to create a revocable trust of the property described in Schedule A hereto annexed, together with such assets as the Trustee may hereafter at any time hold or acquire hereunder (hereinafter referred to collectively as the 'Trust Estate"), for the purpose hereinafter set forth:

NOW, THEREFORE, in consideration of the premises and of the mutual covenants herein contained, the Grantor agrees to execute such

114

further instruments as shall be necessary to vest the Trustee with full title to the property, and the Trustee agrees to hold the Trust Estate, IN TRUST, NEVERTHELESS, for the following uses and purposes and subject to the terms and conditions hereinafter set forth:

The trustee shall hold, manage, invest and reinvest the Trust Estate (if any requires such management and investment) and shall collect the income, if any, there-from _and shall dispose of the net income and principal as follows:_

_I_

DUTIES

NET INCOME

1) During the lifetime of the Grantor, the Trustee shall pay to or apply for the benefit of the Grantor all the net income from the Trust.

PRINCIPAL

2) During the lifetime of the Grantor, the Trustee may pay to or apply for the benefit of the Grantor such sums from the principal of this Trust as in its sole discretion shall be necessary or advisable from time to time for the medical care, comfortable maintenance

and welfare of the Grantor, taking into consideration to the extent the Trustee deems advisable, any other income or resources of the Grantor known to the Trustee.

POWER OF GRANTOR TO WITHDRAW

3) The Grantor may at any time during his lifetime and from time to time, withdraw all or any part of the principal of this Trust, free of trust, by delivering an instrument in writing duly signed by him to the Trustee, describing the property or portion thereof desired to be withdrawn. Upon receipt of such instrument, the Trustee shall thereupon convey and deliver to the Grantor, free of trust, the property described in such instrument.

INABILITY OF GRANTOR

4) In the event that the Grantor is adjudicated to be incompetent or in the event that the Grantor is not adjudicated incompetent, but by reason of illness or mental or physical disability is, in the opinion of the Trustee, unable to properly handle his own affairs, then and in that event the Trustee may during the Grantor's lifetime, in addition to the payments of income and principal comprised in for the benefit of the Grantor, pay to or apply for the benefit of anyone or

116

more of the Grantor's husband/wife and the Grantor's minor children such sums from the net income and from the principal comprised in this Trust in such shares and proportions as in its sole discretion it shall determine to be necessary or advisable from time to time for the medical care, COMFORTABLE maintenance and welfare of the Grantor's said husband/wife and children taking into consideration to the extent the Trustee deems advisable, any other income or resources of the Grantor's said husband/wife and minor children known to the Trustee.

INTERESTS OF GRANTOR

5) The interests of the Grantor shall be considered primary and superior to the interests of any beneficiary.

II

RIGHT OF GRANTOR TO MODIFY AGREEMENT

The Grantor reserves and shall have the exclusive right at any time and from time to time during his/her lifetime by instrument in writing signed by the Grantor and delivered to the Trustee to modify or alter this Agreement, in whole or in part without the consent of the Trustee or any beneficiary provided that the duties, powers and liabilities of the Trustee shall not be changed without his/her consent; and the Grantor reserves and shall have the right during his/her lifetime, by instrument in writing, signed by the Grantor delivered to the Trustee, to cancel and annul this Agreement without the consent of the Trustee or any beneficiary hereof. Grantor expressly reserves the right to appoint successor trustees, replace present trustees and change the beneficiaries or the rights to property due to any beneficiary.

III

POWERS OF TRUSTEE/S

The powers of the trustees will be those granted under applicable law.

IV

DEATH OF GRANTOR

Upon the death of the Grantor, or the last surviving Grantor if more than one, the remaining Trust assets shall be distributed to the beneficiaries in the proportionate or allocable amounts as are specified in the schedule of beneficiaries as may then be in force.

If any beneficiary and the Grantor should die under such circumstances as would render it doubtful whether the beneficiary of the Grantor died first, then it shall be conclusively presumed for the purposes of this Trust that said beneficiary predeceased the Grantor.

V

PERPETUITIES/REMOTENESS

If it shall be determined that any provision of the Trust created herein violates any rule against perpetuities or remoteness of vesting now or hereafter in effect in a governing jurisdiction, that portion of the Trust herein created shall be administered as herein provided until the termination of the maximum period allowed by law at which time and forthwith such part of the Trust shall be distributed in fee simple to the beneficiaries then entitled to receive income there-from.

VI

NO ASSIGNMENTS OR PLEDGE BY BENEFICIARY

Except as otherwise provided herein, all payments of principal and income payable, or to become payable to the beneficiary of any trust created hereunder shall not be subject to assignment, pledge, sale or transfer in any manner, nor shall any said beneficiary have the power to anticipate or encumber such interest, nor shall such interest, while in possession of the Trustee, be liable for, or subject to, the debts, contracts obligations, liabilities or torts of any beneficiary.

VII

This Trust Agreement shall be construed, regulated and governed by and in accordance with the laws of _____.

I certify that I have read the following Trust Agreement and that it correctly states the terms and conditions under which the trust Estate is to be held, managed and disposed of by the trustee.

Dated: _____

Grantor: _____

Trustee: _____

Witness: _____

CHAPTER 14

GLOSSARY OF TERMS

Absolute: Complete and unconditional (1) A rule or order which is complete and becomes of full effect at once, e.g. decree absolute, charging order absolute, garnishee order absolute.

(2) An estate which is not defeasible before its natural expiration.

Absolute Assignment: An assignment of a whole debt, free from conditions but including an assignment by way of trust.

Absolute interest: Full and complete ownership; a vested right of property which is liable to be determined only by the failure of appropriate successors in title.

Accumulation: The continual increase of principle by the reinvestment of interest. Accumulation of income is usually restricted to:

a) The life of the settlor; b) 21 years thereafter; c) The duration of the minority of any person or persons who would have been entitled to the income if of full age d) A term of 21 years from the date of making the disposition.

Action personalis moritur cum persona: (A personal action dies with the person). No executor or administrator could sue or be sued for any tort committed against, or by the deceased in his lifetime.

Active trust: A trust calling for actual duties by the trustee.

Administration of estates: The collection of the assets of a deceased person, payments of debts and distribution of the surplus to the persons beneficially entitled to the deceased's personal representative.

Administration power of: Trustees of trusts may apply capital moneys for the advancement of or benefit, as they thing fit, of any person entitled to the trust property.

Agreement: The concurrence of two or more persons in affecting or altering their rights and duties. An agreement is an act in the law whereby two or more persons declare their consent as two any act or anything to be done or forborne by some or one of those persons for the benefit of others or other of them. Such declaration may take place by (a) the concurrence of the parties in a spoken or written form of words as expressing their common intention, (b) an offer made by some one of them and accepted by the others or other of them (Pullock). The requisites of an agreement are: two or more persons, a distinct intention common to both, known to both, referring to legal relations and affecting the parties (Anson).

Alteration: A material alteration of an instrument, e.g. an alteration of the date of a bill of exchange whereby payment would be accelerated, invalidates the instrument. Alterations in deeds are presumed to have been made before execution in wills, after, and are ignored unless duly executed of the will.

Ambulatory: Revocable for the time being; a provision whose operation is suspended until the happening of some event upon which the provision becomes operative and binding.

Appointment, power of: A power given by a deed or will, to appoint a person to take an estate or interest in property, whether real or personal.

Autre droit (In right of another): E.g. an executor holds the deceased's property in right of the persons entitled to his estate.

Beneficiaries: Persons for whose benefit property is held by trustees.

Chattel is any property other than freehold land. Leasehold and other interests in land less than freehold are termed chattels real, as they savour of the reality. Chattels personal are movable, tangible articles of property.

Codicil: An instrument executed by a testator for adding to, altering explaining or confirming a will previously made by him.

Constructive trust: The person deemed to be a trustee in the case of a constructive trust.

Constructive trustee: A trustee who has the custody and care of trust property, but not its management.

Cy-pres: The doctrine that where a settlor has expressed a general intention, and also a particular way in which he wishes it carried out, but the intention cannot be carried out in that particular way, the court will direct the intention to be carried out as nearly as possible in the way desired.

Declaration of use or trust: A statement or admission that property is to be held to the use of or upon trust for a certain person.

Donatio mortis causa: A gift of personal property in anticipation of death. To be a valid gift it must be made in contemplation of the donors death, be intended to take effect on his death from his existing illness, and be completed by delivery at the time to the donee.

Executor: The person to whom the execution of a will, that is, the duty of carrying its provisions into effect, as required by the testator.

Executor de son tort. (Of his own wrong): One who, being neither executor nor administrator, inter meddles with the goods of the deceased: renders himself liable, not only to an action by the rightful executor or administrator, but also to be sued by a creditor or legatee of the deceased.

Fiduciary: The relationship of one person to another, where the former is bound to exercise rights and powers in good faith, for the benefit of the latter, e.g. as between trustee and beneficiary.

Heir apparent: A person who will be heir to his ancestor if he survives him.

Holograph: A deed or will written entirely by the grantor or testator himself.

Implied trust: A trust implied by law as founded upon the unexpressed but presumed intention of the party. It includes resulting trusts and constructive trusts.

In autre droit (In the right of another): An executor hold property in the right of his testator.

In commendam (In trust).

Inheritance: An estate in land which descends from a man to his heirs.

Judicial trustee: A trustee appointed by the court.

Life Estate: A "mere" freehold, as not being an estate of inheritance. It arises by grant or operation of law for the benefit of a person for the rest of his life.

Overriding trust: A trust which takes precedence of other trusts previously declared.

Perpetuity: A disposition of property by which its absolute vesting is postponed forever. Perpetuities are contrary to the policy of the law, because the "tie up" property and prevent its free alienation. The rule against perpetuities forbids any disposition by which the absolute vesting of property is or may be postponed beyond the period of the life or lives of any number of persons living at the time of the disposition, and further period of years after the death of the survivor, with the possible addition of the period of gestation.

Power: The ability conferred on a person by the donor to determine the legal relations of himself or other. General powers are those which are by law incident or an office: e.g. of solicitor or trustee.

Power of appointment: A power which enables the donee to create or modify estates or interests in property. It confers the right of alienation as opposed to that of enjoyment.

Probate: It is a certificate granted by the court to the effect that a will of a certain person has been proved and registered in court and that administration of his effects has been granted to the executor proving the will, he having first sworn faithfully to administer them and to exhibit a true inventory and render a just account when called on.

Protective Trust: A trust for life, or any less period, of the beneficiary, which is to be determined in certain events such as the bankruptcy of the beneficiary, whereupon the trust income is to be applied for the maintenance, etc. of the beneficiary and his family at the absolute discretion of the trustees.

Public trustee: The official appointed under the Public Trustee act. He is a corporation sole, and state is responsible for his breaches of trust. He may act as a custodian, ordinary or judicial trustee, either solely jointly.

Quasi trustee: A person who, without authority, has taken it on himself to act as a trustee, and he is held liable as though he were a trustee.

Resulting trust: An implied trust where the beneficial interest in property comes back, or results, to the person (or his representatives) who transferred the property to the trustee or provided the means of obtaining it.

Secret trusts: Where there is a bequest or device of property by a testator to a person who has expressly or impliedly agreed to hold the property in trust for another or others, that person will be compelled to carry out the trust. If the testator gives the property to A with an express direction in the will itself that A is to hold upon trust without the trust being disclosed by any will or codicil, A must carry out the trust communicated to him before or at the time of the making of the will (Re Blackwell 1929 A.C. 318). A secret trust is not enforced unless communicated in the testator's lifetime; it must be definite and not illegal.

Statutory trusts: Land held upon the "statutory trusts" is held upon trust to sell and stand possessed of the net proceeds of the net rents and profits until sale after payment of rates, taxes, cost of insurance, repairs, and other outgoings, upon such trusts and subject to such trusts powers and provisions, as may be requisite for giving effect to the rights of the persons interested in land.

Trust: A relation or association between one person (or persons) on the one hand and another person (or persons) on the other, based on confidence, by which property is vested in or held by the one person on behalf of and for the benefit or another.

Trust corporation: The public trustee or a corporation either appointed by the court in any particular case, or entitled by rules made under Public Trustee Act to act as a custodian trustee.

Trust instrument: The instrument whereby the trusts of settled land are declared.

Trustee: A person who holds property in trusts for another.

Trustee de son tort: One who intermeddles in a trust without authority, and is held liable to account as a trustee.

Trustee in bankruptcy: A person in whom the property of a bankrupt is vested for the creditors; his duty is to discover, realise and distribute it among the creditors and for that purpose to examine the bankrupt's property, accounts, etc. to investigate proofs mad by creditors, and to admit, reject or reduce them according to circumstances (Bankruptcy Legislation).

Trustee savings banks: Banks for the deposit of small savings at interest.

Vesting declaration: A declaration in a deed of appointment of new trustees by the appointer that any estate or interest in the trust property is to vest in the new trustees.

Vesting order: An order of a court under which property passes as effectually as it would under conveyance e.g. vesting property in tustees.

CHAPTER 15

THE INTERNATIONAL SCENE

Australia, Canada New Zealand USA have trust laws that are heavily derived from the laws of England. English Trust Law principals therefore predominate in these countries with some exceptions:

Australia

Inter Vivos trusts are created by settlement of a nominal sum of money. (This is not the case for trusts provided for in a will.

Canada

Each province has statutes dealing with the administration of trusts.

With regard to perpetuity law, legislation authorizes trust instruments to last for 80 years. Manitoba has no perpetuity rule.

New Zealand

Since there is no estate duty or capital gains tax discretionary trusts are more common than fixed trusts for asset protection succession planning and flexibility.

Trusts are created by deed and formalities of a deed are that the deed must be executed by all parties to be bound and signatures must be witnessed

South Africa

In this country trust rules are a mixture of English, Roman, Dutch and South African rules.

The trustee is subject to public supervision and is appointed the master of the high court.

There are no perpetuity rules.

The Law reform scene in Canada

There is a move to broaden the understanding of trust use because they can be an estate planning tool for many families.

Exemption Clauses

There is a move to remove disclaimers, wherein trustees attempt to exempt themselves from liability but honest mistakes should be allowed, and such clause should be brought to the attention of clients. Gross negligence should not be allowed.

Fee caps should be lifted but fees should be fair and reasonable

Interim compensation should be allowed but generally courts do not allow this.

Bona fide discretionary allocations should be allowed for beneficiaries not provided for

Majority rule of trustees should be allowed

When public money is raised for, say, a deformed child from Vietnam it was not a charitable trust but the court should be allowed to use it for charitable purposes

Should have a common definition of a spouse like a two year "marriage-like relationship"

More powers should be given to trustees in changed circumstances. Eg if a beneficiary has a spouse etc the trustee should be allowed to exercise by way of a sub-trust or otherwise if the trustee considers the circumstances appropriate, in favour of that spouse.

A transfer must not be made so as to prejudice any person entitled to any prior life or interest

Saunders vs. Vautier should be extended to provide for "variation" not just "termination"

CHAPTER 16

CONCLUSIONS

As of July 29, 1997 in the UK there were nearly 200,000 charitable trusts with assets worth billions of pounds. More than £600 billion in company pensions was under trust management in 200,000 schemes administered by 250,000 trustees.

The courts invented the notion of trusts in England. A Victorian Judge said "A Trustee had to be honest and reasonably competent".

Today Charles Harpum a Law Commissioner and Cambridge academic has said:

"The old picture of the family trust with an avuncular (resembling an uncle) trustee who had lots of spare time to devote to the running of the trust and a range of trustee investments that consisted only of government stocks and mortgages is long dead. The modern trustee needs professional help to steer through the thicket of modern investment practice and to ensure that it is properly managed to secure the best return for the beneficiaries or purposes of the trust"

Many take on the role of trustee without even realising it i.e. a member or the Board of Governors of a private school or the executors of someone's will (1).

The lessons one can learn from the above trend in England are:

1. Trusts have been growing in importance and there is no reason why this will not be the case in Kenya.
2. Trust management requires expertise. It is important that trustees and potential trustees should know their rights, powers and obligations.

CHAPTER 17

DISPUTE RESOLUTION

It is a fact of life in this day and age that disputes do take place between individuals. The types of issues that can result from inheritance matters are manifold. But disputants have become very disillusioned with court-based litigation. The court system is based on the concept of compulsion; the parties are required to attend before a judge who may not be familiar with the technicalities of the dispute. They have to attend a court room in a building with facilities for waiting which neither party would have chosen. They and their legal advisors are obliged to obey a strict form of procedure, which again neither party may have chosen. Cases are usually held in public and so the press may report the proceedings when often the parties prefer privacy. The parties are made to observe a timetable, which places judges' time as having priority over that of the disputants.

Therefore the characteristics of the court system providing compulsion, hearings I public, rigid procedures, and unfriendly timetables are daunting when there have alternatives. This brings to mind the age-old debate about state owned industries with their monopolistic position, their inefficient bureaucracies, and unsuitability to the modern age.

One should look at Alternate dispute resolution systems (ADR) like mediation and arbitration.

There will of course continue to be cases which will have to go through the courts and since there are going to be at least two parties to a dispute the starting point must be to attract them to the private sector.

Arbitrators provide an invaluable public service and at the same time earning the respect not only of the people they serve but also of the government.

Arbitration involves submitting a case to a third party and justice is imposed on them and some parties prefer this. Those that don't like this other appropriate methods such as mediation will continue to develop and grow.

So what is Arbitration?

In its simplest form it is a means for resolving disputes between parties and it exists to give the same result as a court case—Justice.

What are the advantages /

Privacy. It is a private affair and only the parties and the arbitrator are entitled to be present

Simplicity. The way in which proceedings can be conducted can be adapted to suit the needs of the case.

Convenience. This can be conducted to suit the convenience of the parties and the arbitrator

Cost Arbitration should show savings in terms of cost over court actions partly because of the reduced disruption to normal business.

Speed. This can be achieved but requires the co-operation of all the parties to the dispute.

Relationship of the parties. Disputes can be stressful and tiring. It can lead to bad blood. ADR systems can allow people to co-exist and continue in business with each other.

What is mediation?

In this process a neutral person assists the parties to a dispute in reaching their own settlement. This neutral person does not have the authority to make a binding decision on the parties. As the process is voluntary the parties may withdraw from the process at any time.

In contrast arbitration is a process in which each party presents its case at a hearing before a panel of one or more persons who make a binding decision.

Mediation usually precedes arbitration

APPENDIX
FOREWORD

HON. AMOS WAKO, EGH, EBS, MP
ATTORNEY-GENERAL

9From my earlier edition of the book (The law of Trusts in Kenya)

"This handbook manual is a simple general restatement of the law of trusts. In it, the author has in straightforward language highlighted the importance of trusts in modern society and has explicitly compared and contrasted them with wills. What is also contained is a look at other concepts and principles which have an impact on the complex law of trust. The essential elements of a trust are also explained.

Categorization of trusts into constructive, discretionary, protective, fully secret, half secret, resulting and charitable trusts is also concisely dealt with. Mutual Wills are dealt with together with secret Appointment, retirement, removal of trustees, powers, of trustees and investment duties of trustees are explained. The importance of trust corporations in rendering executor and trustee services is also dealt with. Trusts in customary law are in an outline form dealt with in the concluding chapter.

All this is dealt with in simple straightforward language in the handbook manual and is therefore useful in a study of trusts. Although it dies not have adequate reference of municipal legal decisions, it has a wealth of illustrative Commonwealth legal decisions. I therefore recommend this handbook as useful for law students and paralegal officers and in particular all those engaged in the provision of trustee services. This handbook is also suitable for all those studying law as an optional curricula subject and is a simple guide for the legal practitioner at the Chancery bench."

WILLS

CHAPTER 18

INTRODUCTION

PREFACE

There seemed to be a need for an introductory background to the making and revoking of wills in an international context. It would also be useful to the enlightened and industrious law person who would like an insight into this subject. In fact, if there were a profession like an International "Wills Practitioner", this would be the ideal reference book for him or for her.

I have tried to use plain English and to briefly explain all the technical words.

I have not cluttered the book with various citations of authorities. Rather, I have given all the authorities as footnotes so that someone who does not want to be bothered with this can just ignore the footnotes.

On the other hand, the serious reader might want to know on what basis certain proposition are made. And since the UK is the source of trust and succession law for all countries historically

144

connected to it, UK precedents have been used. It has persuasive authority in these countries where laws in this field have evolved.

I have included, in the chapters on The International scenes, summaries of the law in most of these countries.

I have included, at the end of each section, a glossary of legal terms.

TWO CLASSIC WILLS

From the will of a Philadelphia industrialist who died in 1947 . . .

"To my wife I leave her lover, and the knowledge that I wasn't the fool she thought I was.

"To my son I leave the pleasure of earning a living. For twenty-five years he thought the pleasure was mine. He was mistaken.

"To my daughter I leave $100,000. She will need it. The only piece of business her husband ever did was to marry her.

"To my valet I leave the clothes he has been stealing from me for ten years. Also the fur coat he wore last winter while I was in Palm Beach.

"To my Chauffeur I leave my cars. He almost ruined them and I want him to have the satisfaction of finishing the job.

"To my partner, I leave the suggestion that he take some clever man in with him at once if he expects to do any business."

Otto G. Ritcher, Who died in 1960, disposed of six million dollars by a will scrawled on a hospital chart.

The petticoat will was filled for probate in a Los Angeles Court and the trial that ensued to determine that validity of the nurses claim attracted national attention. The jury declared the will genuine but the judge ruled that it was null and void on a technicality: (An individual named in a will cannot also act as a witness.)

CHAPTER 19

SUMMARY

This section first discusses Concepts and Principles of Law and the Nature and Characteristics of Wills.

It then goes on to discuss Will Substitutes like gifts made in contemplation of death, nominations (where property nominated under, are effective irrespective of a Will, joint tenancies (again where property devolves irrespective of a Will), it then discusses conditional Wills (operative only if death occurs in a specified way) and joint Wills. Lastly in this section, mutual Wills and contracts to leave property by will is discussed.

In the next chapter the important topic on the capacity to make wills is discussed, the main issues being that the person must be an adult and must not be of unsound mind, must not have an "insane delusion" and the will must not be held void because of "undue influence". This chapter then goes to discuss fraud and mistake. All these situations are fully explained in this section.

The next chapter discusses the formalities requested to make wills, showing examples of how incorrectly completed wills have been held to be void.

The booklet then discusses how wills are revoked, again giving examples from decided cases showing how Wills are revoked indicating when revocations are invalid. This chapter then discusses revocation by marriage (still valid).

The following chapter discusses a few small topics like revival of wills as well as oral wills.

Then comes a discussion the important provision that has to be made for dependents, explaining who is a "dependent", under "Can a testator/testatrix disinherit a dependent?"

Following this comes a discussion on how gifts can fail when the gift is converted to something else, or if the beneficiary predeceases the testator.

The next chapter discusses the important issue as to what happens during intestacy (when a will is not made) or partial intestacy (when the will does not deal with certain dispositions). It gives examples of how property is distributed, depending on who survives the deceased (e.g.

spouse and children, spouse and no child, child/
ren but no spouse, and no spouse or child/ren).

Reference has been made to peculiarities in the
law for each country that has had historical
ties to the UK, as well as the law reform scene in
Canada.

The international scene is discussed followed by,
in the "conclusions" a discussion of the Trusts
and estates Practitioner, a discussion on burials,
living wills and human Genetic Intervention.

CHAPTER 20

WHAT IS A WILL?

A will has been defined as the declaration by a person of his wishes or intentions regarding the disposition of his/her property after death, duly made and executed (1).

A Will therefore helps protect the people you care about. It spells out your wishes so that your family members do not have to make decisions they feel uncomfortable with. It will save them the added grief when they need it least.

If you die without leaving a will, the laws of the country will determine what happens to your property after death. The process is lengthy, time consuming, and your relatives may never get what they need or you anticipated they would get.

The Act also has a provision for "privileged" wills which can be oral if made by the members of the armed forces of the Merchant Marine during a period of active service and if made within three months of dying.

There are other laws and legal principles that impact upon matters of succession. Examples are Trust Law, Equity, and the Law of Co-ownership, Nominations, and Perpetuities & Accumulations.

MAKING A WILL

When you die, your property (called your estate) must be properly administrated. Affairs must be wound up, property and possessions passed to relatives or friends or sold debts and funeral expenses paid, and heirs given the benefits intended for them. A Will ensures all this is done quickly and properly, in accordance with your wishes.

When you make your will you choose your executors whom you wish to administer your estate, people who can be relied upon to carry out your wishes with understanding and compassion. Your advocate or trust corporation could be one of the executors and can normally start administering your estate almost immediately after your death, but nothing can be disposed of until probate is granted, except property held jointly with a spouse.

You can leave your property and possessions to whomever you wish subject to the legal rights of certain family members. You can leave selected objects (furniture, jewels, paintings, stamp collections, antiques etc) to particular family members or friends or to charities.

It is important to remember that the sale price of your house or flat, and any other property you own, including your stock and shares, and your savings in a bank or building society, will add to the size of your estate.

Your advocate will usually advise you how best to write your will so that distribution is exactly as you desire. You may decide, for simplicity's sake to divide your entire estate into equal portions giving one part to a relative, one part to a friend and one part to your favorite charity.

You may prefer to specify the amount to benefit particular family members and friends.

Whatever you decide, it is essential you include the residue (i.e. all that is left after specified bequests have been made) and that you say clearly how you want the residue to be distributed. This is normally done by allocating the whole of the residue to one person or to a charity, or by splitting it into equal portions, giving individuals or charities a portion of each.

Unless you have mastered the principles behind making Wills—Do consult your advocate or trust corporation. Your intentions may be very simple, but the legal formalities and language required are complicated and need to be strictly followed. What may appear to be a trivial difference in wording could make a major difference legally.

There are several reasons given why people do not make Wills:

"It is all too legal and I do not understand it"

"It is a chore—I will put it off until next month"

"If I make a Will, I am tempting fate"

"I do not like seeing advocates"

"Making a Will costs too much"

"I might change my mind and want the Will altered"

"I have nothing worth leaving"

On the other hand recommendations in this book are quite simple. You must make a proper will.

Advocates make far more money sorting out problems where there is no Will, or sorting out badly made wills. Making a Will usually creates fewer complications after your death, and allows you to include charities in your specific wishes.

In short, even though there is no legal obligation to make a will, the cost of making one is not high, especially compared with the headache and confusion that may be caused after your death if you leave no Will or a badly drafted will.

In this book, however, some guidelines are given as to the principles involved in relation to Wills and if these principles are followed, chances are that a simple home-made Will may be valid.

Generally, the Law of Succession is affected by other Laws e.g. the Law of Immovable Property (Land Law), the Law and Form of Marriage (Family Law), the Law of Contract, Equity and other forms of Common Law.

Questions that often come to the mind of a property owner are:

What is Succession to property; is it the same as inheritance?

"Succession is said to take place where property passes on the death of someone, to his successor.

Inheritance, however, is an estate in land which devolves from someone to his heirs.

Succession therefore refers to any form of property (e.g. personal effects, cars etc) while inheritance only refers to land.

There are obviously, therefore, different forms of succession. Succession can be "testate" where one leaves a Will or "intestate" where one does not leave a Will. Again succession of the land is different from; say succession of personal effects.

Law, as long as it was not inconsistent with any other statute of general application.

Different forms of property are subject to different rules and regulations on succession.

Succession to immovable property in a will shall be regulated by the law of the place where it was siuated, whatever the domicile of that person at the time of his death.

On the other hand, succession to movable property should be regulated by the Law of Domicile of that person at the time of his death.

Domicile means:

The country in which a person is, or presumed to be, a permanently resident. The place of a person's permanent home.

A person who, immediately before his death, was ordinarily resident in a country, shall be presumed to have been domiciled in that country, at the date of his death, (In the absence of proof of domicile elsewhere).

CHAPTER 21

THE NATURE AND CHARACTERISTICS OF A WILL AS A LEGAL DEVICE

In short, a Will is a document in writing, signed in accordance with certain formalities by which a person disposes of his property to take effect after his death. Such a document contains statements regarding the disposition of a person's property on death and is subject to a process called "probate". What all this implies is that if someone wants to leave property to certain named individuals or organizations he or she will have to have a document prepared in a particular way and sign it as well as witness it, in a particular way.

Such a system laid out according to law of the land validates a will. If someone dies having made a valid Will, he or she has died "testate". If no will was made the person will have died "intestate".

It is very important that someone make a will because, when someone dies intestate either the spouse or one or more children (i.e. persons entitled to succeed on action) has to provide a surety bond twice in value of the estate. This is usually from a financial institution like an insurance company or bank.

If there is a dispute amongst the potential beneficiaries or when there is no one willing or able to take out letters, the property goes under the control of the pubic Trustees. Therefore, it is a very difficult process for one to undergo if there is no will at least to ensure that the spouse and children get what is rightfully theirs. This difficulty is not confined to Kenya. Even in the UK, it has been a nightmare until recently, if the head of the family dies intestate.

Some of the characteristics of a will are as follows:-

Wills do not only confine themselves to the disposition of property. They also appoint trustees or executors. These are individuals appointed in the will (or sometimes by the court) to act as personal representatives of the deceased so as to give effect to the will.

A will can consist of one, or several documents. It is always revocable (capable of being cancelled) before death.

It is also ambulatory (i.e. takes effect only on death). There are documents (which we will discuss later) like Mutual Wills and contracts to leave specific property by will which are not consistent with the ambulatory nature of wills.

WILL SUBSTITUTES

There are a number of dispositions that take effect on death but are not exactly wills. They are considered as will substitutes.

DONATIO MORTIS CAUSA

This has been defined [1] as "A singular form of a gift. It may be said to be of amphibious nature, being a gift which is neither entirely inter vivos (a lifetime gift) nor testamentary (a gift effective on death).

It is an act inter vivos by which the donee (recipient) is to have absolute title to the subject matter of the gift not at once but if the donor dies. To make a gift valid it must be made so as to take complete effect on the donor's death. Such dispositions have the following three characteristics:—It must be made in contemplation of death, it must be conditional on death and there must be parting with "domination": i.e. possession".

The best example to illustrate the concept of donation mortis causa would be to refer to a relatively recent case. (2)

A couple had lived as a man and a wife for ten years before separating. They, however, had continued to be on friendly terms, for many years thereafter. The man later contracted cancer and was moved to a hospital.

The woman visited him every day to feed him and give him company. He told her that after his death his house and his contents were to be hers and that the deeds to the house were to be found in a steel box.

The keys to the house were in the possession of the woman, apparently after the man slipped them into her handbag, during one of her visits to him. After his death she claimed that the house was hers on the basis that it was a valid donatio mortis causa. The claim was contested by the next of kin of the deceased.

The court of appeal found in her favour that it was a valid D.M.C as the three essential requirements for such a gift had been satisfied in the case. Therefore she did get the house.

NOMINATIONS

Nominations allow property to pass to someone nominated (as explained later), and this facility operates independently of wills.

On the death of a member, a registered society may transfer the share or interest (e.g. property) of the deceased member to the person nominated in accordance with this and any rules made there under. Nominations have to be made in writing, signed and witnessed by two persons.

COMMON LAW RULES ON NOMINATIONS

It has no effect until the nominator's death, and is revocable (i.e. possible to cancel) until then. (3)

If the person who is nominated (nominee) predeceases (i.e. dies before) the one who nominates him or her then the nomination lapses (fails). (4)

A person can make both a nomination and a will and, provided they deal with different assets, they can operate side by side. (5)

If there is a nomination and a will of the same asset to different persons, the subject matter of the nomination is not affected by the will; the asset goes to the person named in the nomination, as long as the nomination has been validly created. (5.a)

162

Every member of a registered society has to, at the time of becoming a member, nominee in writing (with two attesting witnesses) one person to succeed to the nominators share and interest.

The facts of a recent case (5.b) the deceased had nominated, in accordance with the rules of a pension scheme, his brother as a beneficiary in the event, which eventually happened, of his death in service. Subsequently he married but did not vary or revoke the nomination of his brother as beneficiary.

The widow claimed the nomination was testamentary and since it did not comply with the required formalities for wills, it was invalid.

It was held that the nomination was not testamentary. Accordingly the nomination was valid and the widow's claim failed.

JOINT TENANCIES

Under certain circumstances and can be held by two or more persons under joint tenancies. When land is held this way, there is what is called the right of survivorship, and this is the unique thing about this form of ownership.

The implication of this is that if one joint tenant dies, then the property passes to the remaining joint tenant irrespective of what the will says and there is therefore no need to probate the will or undergo any cumbersome procedures before the property passes on to the remaining Joint Tenants. This is a very useful method for two persons to hold property (usually husband and wife). This type of ownership must be distinguished from Tenancies In Common, where there is no right of survivorship. When a Tenant in Common dies, his interest under his will, or through rules of intestate succession, passes on to the remaining Tenant in Common.

The ownership document will usually stipulate that say A & B hold certain property as "Joint tenants" or "Tenants In Common".

CONDITIONAL WILL

A conditional will is one that is only operative if death occurs in a specific way or period or place.

It has been held that a will worded with the following phrase "If I die before my return from my journey to Ireland" was held to be a conditional will.

164

The will only has effect, therefore, if the person (in the above example) dies on this journey back from Ireland otherwise he would not have had an effective will and would have died intestate.

It must, however, be pointed out that in a situation where there is ambiguity in the wording of such a condition the court usually leans against ruling that it is a conditional will. (7)

JOINT WILL

This is a single document consisting of the will of more than one testator. It is intended to be the will of each person. Therefore if two persons make a joint will and one dies the joint will has effect. Then if the next person dies, that same document is effective as the second persons will. Such wills are usually also mutual wills (see next section).

MUTUAL WILLS

This is a subject of much case law and complexity.

The head note of a leading case, however gives a somewhat comprehensive definition of mutual wills. (8)

This is paraphrased here: Where two persons have made arrangements as to the disposal of their property and executed mutual wills in pursuance of those arrangements, the one of them who predeceases (dies before) the other, dies with the implied promise of the one who survives that the said arrangements will be binding in him. And, if the survivor, after taking a benefit under the arrangements, alters his will, the personal representative of the said survivor who dies, is obliged to carry out the contract or arrangement made, when they were both alive. This is because the will of the one who has died first has, by the death, become irrevocable.

Thus for example H arranges with his wife W that they will do a mutual will so that whoever dies, the surviving spouse will hold the assets during her or his life time, after which their son inherits the assets.

If, say H dies after such a mutual will is validly made, W cannot then make a will leaving the assets to say, her sister. She is bound to leave the assets to their son.

A mutual will can be in the form of a joint will i.e. on one document. It is usual, if the wills are on separate documents to be dated the same day.

The effect of the mutual wills is that if they are held to be mutual, the survivor is bound (under contract and trust principles) to carry out the arrangements.

In one modern leading case (9), a husband and wife made wills on the same day in the same terms but no agreement was mentioned in either of the wills.

It was held that there was a mutual will because of the various statement made by the wife who survived. It was emphasized in this case that the mere facts that the wills were simultaneously executed was not in itself conclusive. The relevant circumstances were important considerations.

In another case (10), a husband and wife made a joint will in which it was expressly stated that the parties had agreed to dispose of their property in the manner described therein and that there was to be no alteration or revocation of the document without agreement.

This was held to be a mutual will, and the surviving spouse was bound.

CONTRACTS TO LEAVE PROPERTY BY WILL

A will is always revocable even if it states that it is irrevocable. However, a testator may make a contract to make certain provisions for certain pensions in his will.

Thus, for example, the testator may promise to leave his girlfriend his house in his will, should she marry him. This can be a binding contract.

Regardless of the nature of the contract, the will can still be revoked (i.e. a new will with terms different from the contractual terms). If, however, the will is revoked in this way there will be a breach of contract.

It has been held that provided there is a legally binding contract, the disappointed beneficiary will be able to sue for damages for breach of contract should the testator fail to honor his or her promise.

If the contract is to leave specified property by will, the disappointed beneficiary can sue on the contract before the testator has disposed of the property in a manner which puts it beyond the testator's power to make the agreed provision [11].

It has been held the court even has the power to order that specific property promised by the will be transferred to the person who has been promised, where this is a possibility. [12]

It will also be seen in the section on Concepts and Principles of law how Trusts and Equity impact upon the law of succession. In brief, a trust is created when a mutual will is made. A trust can also be created on the death of a testator for the benefit of his or her children or for persons of unsound mind.

Equity plays an important role in succession law.

Injunctions are equitable remedies and can be obtained in succession proceedings in the court.

The maxims of equity (e.g. "He who seeks equity must do equity", "He who comes to equity must come with clean hands", "Where the equities are equal, the law prevails"), all apply in succession proceedings.

For further insight into "Equity" see concepts and principles of law".

---

(1)Re Beaumont 1902 86 L.T 410

(4)Re. Barnes (1940) ch 276; 109 L.J ch 102; 162 L.T 263

(5a) Barnet V. Slater

(5b) Baird V. Baird 1990

(6)Parsons Vs Lanoe (1748) 1 Ves. 189; 1 Wils. 243

(7)In the Goods of Spratt (1897) P. 28; 66 L.J.P. 25; 75L. T. 518

(8)Stone V Hoskins (1905) P. 194; 74 L.J. P 110; 93 L.T441;S4WR 64

(9)Re.Cleaver (Dec'd) 1981 1 WR 939; (1981) 2 All E.R 1018

(10)Re. Hagger (Dec'd) 1930 2 CH 190; 99 L.J. CH 492; L.T. 610

(11)Hammersley V de biel (1845) 12 CL & FIN.45; 8ER 1312

(12)Synge V Synge (1894) 1QB. 466; (1891-94) All E REP 1164

(13)MILNES V FODEN (1890) 15 PD 105

(14)DOUGLAS—MENZIES V UMPHELBY (1908) AC 224, 233

CHAPTER 22

CAPACITY

MINORS

No person under the age of 18 can make a valid will. [1]

UNSOUNDNESS OF MIND

Any person making a will shall be deemed of sound mind unless, at the time of executing the will, is in such a state of mind, whether arising from mental or physical illness, drunkenness or from any other cause, as not to know what he or she is doing [2].

Therefore a person must be of sound mind when executing a will. This was explained in a well known English case. [3] "It is essential to the exercise of such a power that a testator shall understand the nature of the act and its effect; shall understand the extent to which he is disposing; shall be able to comprehend and appreciate the claims to which he ought to give effect; and with a view to the latter objects that no disorder of the mind shall poison his affections, pervert his sense of right, or prevent the exercise of his natural facilities—that no insane delusion shall influence his will in disposing of his property, and bring about a disposal of it which, if the mind has been sound, would not have been made".

INSANE DELUSION

Insane delusions are a classical example of a form of mental illness which may not affect the testator's ability to make a will.

It has been held that where a delusion has had, or is calculated to have had, an influence on the testamentary disposition it must be held to be fatal to its validity. (4)

In a well known case, since 1841 the testator had illusions that he was being molested by a man who was long dead and he was being pursued by evil spirits.

He had been confined to an asylum on several occasions. In 1863 the testator made a will and died in 1865 at which time he was still afflicted by his delusions. It was held that the will was valid because the delusions would not have had any effect on the disposition of the property made by the testator.

172

On the other hand, in another case (5) the testator left a will which excluded his only daughter of any benefit.

Evidence showed that he had an irrational aversion for his daughter and refused to see her for the first three years of her life. It was in this case, held that the will could not stand. The delusion had a direct effect on the disposition in the will.

If a man believes he is Napoleon Bonaparte, and leaves his estate to his wife, despite the delusion he has still left his estate to his wife and so the will stands.

The nature of the testators' afflictions may be such that it only affects certain dispositions in the will. In such circumstances the will will be admitted to probate minus the affected parts (6).

An interesting recent case, showing what "insane delusions" can result in was when a testator made a will leaving the major part of his estate to his son.

He was then admitted to hospital and became very ill. When his son visited him, the testator formed the delusion that his son was trying to kill him.

This was because the son tried to push back his father to the pillow to help his breathing.

Laboring under this delusion, the testator made another will in which he revoked the previous gift to the son. The son claimed that the first will was still valid as the subsequent will was under a delusion.

It was held that the second testamentary document could not stand and was invalid on account of the father's unfounded belief that the son was attempting to shorten his life. (7)

If the will is rational in the face of it, and duly executed, there is presumption that the testator had the necessary mental capacity and the will will be considered valid.

In these circumstances, it will be necessary for any party who wishes to challenge the validity of the will (on the grounds that the testator lacked the requisite mental capacity) to adduce evidence to rebut this presumption (i.e. to show he was not of sound mind).

The burden of proof that a testator was, at the time he made any will, not of sound mind shall be upon the person who so alleges. (8)

Therefore it is the person who alleges that the testator was of unsound mind to prove that the testator was of unsound mind.

174

There is a presumption that a person who lacked testamentary capacity at some time before the execution of the will continued to lack testamentary capacity at the date of the execution. (9)

However, when the testator had the requisite capacity before executing his will, there is a presumption that he or she continued to have the ability to make a will until the contrary is proven. (10)

UNDUE INFLUENCE

A will of any part, the making of which of has been caused by fraud or coercion (force or compulsion) or by such importunity (soliciting pressingly) as takes away the free agency of the testator, is void (11).

What amount to undue influence which is enough to invalidate a will has been explained in an old case by Sir JP Wilde (12).

"In a word, a testator may be led but not driven, and his will must be the offspring of his own volition and not the record of someone else".

Therefore if the testator is "driven" and the will is the record of someone else—it is undue influence, therefore the will is void.

If violence is threatened against the testator in order to extract a particular will from him, this again amounts to undue influence.

The same would apply if the testator is confined to a locked room, starved of food or fatigued by incessant talking to him when ill or weak.

However, there will be no undue influence if persuasion or mere influence has been used. Thus a wife or children who impress their moral claim on the testator will not be guilty of having exerted undue influence.

In an old case it was held that an allegation of undue influence had been proved by the party making it where the testator had left substantial part of her estate to a Roman Catholic priest.

Therefore in contrast to undue influence in the law of a contract, there are no situations which raise a presumption of undue influence. (13)

In law of contract undue influence is presumed to have taken place between, say, a lawyer and a client, father and son, and, in the above example the priest and the testator.

UNDUE INFLUENCE AND THE USE OF AN INTERMEDIARY

"Suspicious circumstances" arise in cases where the party preparing the will takes a benefit of himself but it is not confined to such cases.

In an old case it was said to "extend to all cases in which circumstances exist which excite the suspicion of the court". Suspicious circumstances attending the will, puts the burden of proving it on the person who draws up the will and who receives the benefit. If this burden cannot be discharged he would not receive the gift.

In another case the testatrix, aged 82 made a will in favour of a nephew and other relatives, leaving them various houses. In a previous will she had left them to various tenants of these houses.

The later will was made between the testatrix and her solicitor with the nephew's wife conducting the correspondence on behalf of the testator. It was held that this created "suspicious circumstances" and the nephew and relatives did not receive the gifts. (14)

There was a celebrated case where a will prepared by a solicitor under which he took a substantial benefit was ultimately struck down. There was an elderly lady who might be called old, unversed in business having no one upon whom to rely except the solicitor who acted for her and her family. The solicitor made a will for the client under which he took the bulk of her large estate. (15)

Much, however, wills depend on the facts of each case in which suspicious circumstances arise, as to what sort of evidence is required in order to remove the suspicion.

In another case (16) the testator, an elderly man, made his will at the house of his lawyer in the presence of two independent and respectable witnesses. By his will, he left his lawyer a quarter of his estate and left other legacies to friends.

He left nothing to his only son. On the testator's death the son challenged the will on, among other grounds, suspicious circumstances because the will was made in the attorney's own handwriting.

It was held that although suspicion surrounded the gift to the attorney, the court was satisfied that this was removed by evidence being put forward that the testator excluded his son from his will for criminal conduct and because the will was drawn up in the presence of two independent witnesses.

178

FRAUD

A testator will not have the requisite capacity where he has been prompted to make provisions in his will for, or exclude from his will, a beneficiary because of false statements made to him in relation to that beneficiary.

It is often difficult to prove fraud.

In a case [17], a testamentary gift was impaired for fraud when the married beneficiary had induced the gift by saying that she was unmarried and therefore capable of marrying him.

Although the marriage took place it was obviously bigamous and the consequence was that the beneficiary could not receive the gift.

MISTAKE

Mistakes can take many forms, and are here categorized into 3 types:-

Clerical Errors:

The testator or typist might make a slip of the pen or a typing error.

A classical example is from a recent case. [18] The testator made a long and detailed will. Clause 7 contained 20 legacies. Sometime after executing the will, the testator instructed her solicitor to draw up a codicil to revoke the gifts in clause 3 and 7. (iv)

However, owing to a clerical error the codicil was drawn up in the following terms—"I revoke clauses 3 and 7 of my said will". If the codicil were allowed to stand, some [19] other gifts in clause 7 would also be revoked.

It was held that the court had no power to insert the Roman numeral (iv) in the codicil. The court only had the power to omit words from the will or codicil.

Since, however, the manner in which the testator's intention could most nearly be effected was by omitting the reference to clause 7 in the codicil, this was done i.e. clause 7 was allowed to remain in the main will.

Therefore the court would omit words to get nearer to the testators clear intention. [19]

Mistake as to legal effect.

If a testator knew and approved of the inclusion of a particular clause, it will stand even if he was mistaken as to its legal effect.

In a decided case [20] the testator left two wills and a codicil. A revocation clause included in a codicil in fact had the effect of revoking the whole of the earlier will but which the testator was wrongly advised that it revoked only one part of the will. It was held that whole of the will was revoked, contrary to the testators wishes, because he was mistaken as to its legal effect.

Where, however, if a situation arises because of either inadvertence or a misunderstanding i.e. a mistake without the knowledge and approval of the testator, the courts have been held to be more merciful.

In a recent case [21] the testator made a home made will under which his landlady and her husband were the main beneficiaries. He then conceived the notion that his three holdings in unit trusts had to be disposed of by separate wills and he made and executed three more wills in their favour, each will made on a will form at the same time and each disposing of a separate holding.

(1)Wills Act 1837 S7 and Law of Succession Act Cap 160 S5 (1)

(2)Banks V Goodfellow (1870) LR 5QB. 549; 39 L.J QB237

(3)Banks V Goodfellow (1870) LR SQB 549; 39 LJQB 237

(4)Dew V Clerk (1826) 162 ER 410; 3 ADD 79

(5)In the estate of Bohrmann (1938) 1 All ER 271; 158 LT 180

(6)Re. Nightingle (1974) 119 s.j 189

(7))Banks V Goodfellow 91870) LR 5QB 549; 39 LJ QB 237

(8)Parker V Felgate (1883) 32 WR 186; 47 J.P 808

(9) Cap 160 S7

(10)Hall V Hall (1868) 16 WR 544; 32 JP 503; 18 LT 152

(11)Parfitt V Lawless (1872) 21 WR 200; 36 JP 822; 27 LT 215

(12)Tyrell V Painton (1894) 42 WR 343; 6 R 540

(13)Wintle V NYE (1959) 1 WLR 284; (1969) 1 All ER 522

(14)Barry V Butlin (1838) 12 ER 1089; 1 COURT 637

(15)Wilkinson V Joughin

(16)Re. Morris (1971) P62; (1970) 2 WLR 865; (1970) 1 All ER 1057

(17)Re. Reynette—James (1976) 1 WLR 161; (1976) 3 All ER 1037

(18)Collins V Elstone (1893) 9 TLR 16; 41 WR 287

(19)Re. Phelan (1972) FAM 33; (1971) 3 WLR 888

CHAPTER 23

FORMALITIES

No written will shall be valid unless:

> The testator has signed or affixed his mark to the will.

The statutory law in the U.K. is silent on the fact that a "mark" may be used. On the other hand, in a decided U.K case, it was held that the testator, which is intended to be his signature, will suffice. Thus, initials, assumed in a name, a thumbprint or a stamped name were regarded as sufficient.

In another case (2) "servant of Mr. Sperling" were held a sufficient signature.

It is valid if, "the signature or mark of the testator, or the signature of the person signing from him, if so placed that it shall appear that it was intended thereby to give effect to the writing as a will".

In a decided case (3) a signature placed on the left hand margin at right angles to disposition was held void.

In another case (4), a signature placed in a box marked out among dispositive words was held void.

In yet another case (5), the testator signed the will at the top, attested by one witness. The will was then put into the envelope and the testator wrote her name on the envelope and two witnesses also signed the envelope. It was held that it was invalidly executed.

The signature on an envelope is not intended as a signature to the will, but merely as an identification of the document; on the other hand it was decided (6) that the signature of the testator and two other persons on the envelope below the words "last will and testament of J. Mann" was held valid.

The will must have been attested by two or more competent witnesses, each of whom must have seen the testator sign or affix his mark to the will.

If a witness is in another room at a distance of seven yards, it was held that the testator could have seen them sign through a broken window if he so desired and it was held a valid will. (7)

If a will is attested by a witness in a lawyer's office, and the testator is in his carriage outside

184

he could have seen them sign through the windows and it was held a valid will [8].

This expression "in the presence" must be taken to mean visual presence. A will therefore is not validly signed where one of the witnesses was engaged at the time on the other side of the shop with a person who stood between him and the testator [9].

A testatrix, under the influence of drugs and dying signed "E CHAL" instead of "E CHALCRAFT". The witnesses signed immediately.

Although the testator was lapsing into unconsciousness at the time of signing, she was sufficiently mentally present and it was held valid [10].

The will is valid if the witnesses "have seen some other person sign the will, in the presence and by the direction of the testator" or have received from the testator a personal acknowledgment of his signature or mark, or of the signature of the other person.

The will is valid if the witnesses "have seen some other person sign the will, in the presence and by the direction of the testator" or have received from the testator a personal acknowledgement of his signature or mark, or of the signature of that other person.

According to UK statutory law, the two witnesses must be present at the same time.

It is not necessary that the witness be informed that the document being signed is a will because they are attesting the testator's signature and not the will itself. (11)

Further if the testator signs the will in the presence of both witnesses, they need not see the signature. It is sufficient that they see him in the act of signing.

No form of attestation shall be necessary. (12)

Professionally drawn wills, however, invariably include an attestation clause which recited that the formalities have been complied with. Such a clause is desirable because it raises a presumption of due regularity and facilitates the obtaining of probate.

It is essential that all of the dispositive parts of the will have been duly executed and attested and this must be in existence when the will is made. (13)

Therefore a power to incorporate existing documents is recognized provided the documents

186

is in writing, in existence at the date when the will is executed, clearly identified and referred to as an existing document in the will.

LIABILITY FOR NEGLIGENT EXECUTION

A lawyer who negligently supervises or fails to supervise the execution of a will may be liable in negligence to the disappointed beneficiary.

In a famous modern case [14] T (T = Testator) instructed his solicitors to draw up his will in the terms he had given them and when ready for execution to post it to P (the plaintiff) where T was staying. The solicitors sent a covering letter with the will should be executed.

The solicitor, however, failed to inform T that P (who received benefits under the will) could not have her husband sign as a witness.

P (P = Plantiff) sued the solicitor in negligence. It was held, that the solicitor was liable.

RECENT DEVELOPMENTS

ZAVAH

In a recent case [15], a testator had the handwritten document, written in Hebrew and known as "Zavah", a Jewish form of a will. The

Zavah was executed with the formalities required by the Act. At that time the testator was in possession of his last will as we know it but did not sign it until after signing the Zavah.

The said Zavah referred to the will which was wrongly signed, with only one witness.

It was held probate was granted for the Zavah with the will incorporated in it.

In a case decided in 1991 (16) it was held that a signature written in advance of the text of the will could not be regarded as a signature to the will since at that time the document was not a will.

All the Probate & Administration Court has to is to satisfy itself is that the will is valid—not disputes of title to land

---

(1)In the Estate of Cook (1960) 1 WLR 353; (1960) 1 All ER 689

(2)In the Goods of Sperling (1863) 12 WR 354; 9 L.T. 34

(3)Re. Roberts (1934) P. 102

(4)Re. Hornby (1946) P. 171

(5)Re. Beadle (Dec'd) (1974) 1 All E. R 493

(6)Re. Mann (Dec'd) (1942) P. 146

(7)Shires V Glasscock (1688) 2 SALK 688

(8)Casson V Dade (1781) 1 BRO CC. 99

188

(9)Brown V Skirrow (1902) P. 3

(10)In the Goods of Chalcraft (1948) P. 222

(11)Smith V Smith (1866) L.R. 1 P & D. 146

(12)Harris V Knight (1890) 15 PD 170

(13)Re. Smarts Goods (1902) 18 TLR 663; 87 LT 142

(14)Rose V Caunters (1979) 3 WLR 605 (1979) 3 All ER 580

(15)Wood V Smith (1991) 2 All ER 939

(16)Re. Berger (DEC'D) (1989) 1 All ER 591

CHAPTER 24

REVOCATION OF WILLS

A will may be revoked or altered by the maker of it at anytime when he is competent to dispose of his free property by will. No will or codicil or any part thereof shall be revoked otherwise than by another will or codicil declaring an intention to revoke it, or by the burning, tearing, or otherwise destroying of the will with the intention of revoking it, by the testator, or by some other person at his direction.

In a decided case, a testator made a will by which he gave all his property to a named beneficiary.

Subsequently he made another will leaving all his real estate to another named beneficiary and then decided to leave all his property to the beneficiary under the first will and he therefore destroyed in the second will.

This did not amount to revival of the first will which had been revoked by implication by the second will, so far as the disposition of the real estate was concerned. (1)

There has to be an intention to destroy a will, like the statement "go get my will and burn it". [2]

In another decided case [3], in her first will T left her estate upon trust to pay an annuity (a sum payable annually) to her son, H, for life and on his death to be divided equally between her grandchildren on attaining 21 years of age.

In her second will, T left all her estate to her son, H, absolutely (no annuity and no provision for the grandchildren). The absolute gift to H in the second will did not contain a revocation clause. It was held that there was nothing in the second will which revoked the first one in an unqualified manner and so the first will was still valid.

A revocation clause will have no effect if T did not know and approve of its presence. [4] Thus T executed a home-made will in favour of his landlady and later, under a mistaken belief as to the operation of wills, he executed 3 further wills on printed forms disposing of certain holdings. The printed revocation clause at the top of each printed form was not deleted. It was held that all four wills were valid and the revocation clauses in the last 3 wills were omitted.

There can be revocation by destruction of part of the will only, as opposed to the whole will. In

such circumstances if the court is satisfied that
T intended the remainder to be effective, it will
be admitted to probate. In a decided case (5) T
directed that his residuary estate be held in trust
but the parts if the will dealing with the trust
were found cut away at his death. The will was
complete in all other respects. Probate was granted
to an un-mutilated will on the basis that the
trusts had been cut out. This was allowed on the
understanding that there was no indication that
the whole will was intended to be revoked.

In another case (6), a will was found in a
mutilated state, cut and torn at certain points
but with the signature of T and the witness intact.
It was held that the will was revoked in part only.

Revocation by destruction contains two elements,
an act of destruction and an intention to revoke.
(7). In another case (8), part of a will was cut and
the remaining parts stitched together. It was held
that the will was revoked in part only.

It must be remembered, however, that it may be
impossible to draw any conclusion other than
the whole will was intended to be revoked, where
the remainder of the will cannot be understood
without the missing parts.

192

The destruction can be at the act of another, provided it is done in Ts presence and by his direction. Thus if a will is accidentally destroyed by fire, subsequent acquiescence (acceptance as having been destroyed) will not suffice. (9)

A testator also cannot adopt or ratify the act of another (10).

Thus if a testator's will was torn up by his wife in a fit of temper, but was not revoked, there can be no subsequent ratification of this by him. The destruction must therefore be accompanied by the proper authority to revoke it at the time it took place.

Destruction by another must be in Ts presence, there is, however, a decided case that this must be so (11).

In this case T asked one of the executors of her will to take a codicil to the will and destroy it as she no longer wished it to have effect.

The codicil was brought to T who was confined to bed. As there was no fire in the bedroom, it was taken to another room and burned in the presence of the executor and several other persons but not in the presence of T.

It was held that the codicil was not revoked and the executor and the others who knew of its contents were required to give evidence of the terms of the burnt codicil so that they could be admitted to probate.

DEPENDENT RELATIVE REVOCATION

It has long been established by common law that the revocation of the first will is dependant upon the relative validity of the second will which is intended to replace it. If the second will under certain circumstances is not valid, for any reason, the first will may be regarded as not revoked.

In a decided case [12] T instructed his solicitor to draft a new will and at the same time he gave the instructions, he cut his signature in his old will being under the misapprehension that he could not make a new will until the old one has been revoked. He died before he could sign the new will.

It was held that the old will had not been revoked because evidence showed that T would, had it not been for his mistaken belief, have allowed the old will to remain effective up until his new will was executed.

On the other hand, the intention might be to definitely revoke the first will in any case.

In another decided case [13] T made a will in 1965 leaving her small firm to P and his sister. She kept the will in her custody. In 1970 she decided to change her will as P & his sister did not visit her very often, and she made an appointment with her solicitor for this person.

However, before she could keep this appointment she took seriously ill and died. After her death, her will was found mutilated. It was held that the revocation of the will was absolute and unqualified, more so because before she died she said she had no will. Therefore she died intestate.

If a will is destroyed because of mistaken belief by T as to the operation of the law or as to certain facts, this will not amount to revocation. [14]

Conditional revocation may apply to alterations. If a testator obliterates a legacy and substitutes a new legacy which is unattested or pastes a slip of paper over the legacy bearing a new figure, then the old legacy remains effective if it was done in the mistaken belief that the new legacy was effective.

REVOCATION BY MARRIAGE

A will shall be revoked by the marriage of the maker.

Even a voidable marriage will revoke a will. (15)

But where a will is expressed to be made in contemplation of marriage with a specified person, it shall not be revoked by marriage so contemplated.

In a decided case (16) it was held that a will in contemplation of marriage had to be expressed to be in contemplation of marriage and that could be done in one of three ways:

An express clause e.g. "The will is made in contemplation of my forthcoming marriage to X".

Words from which contemplation of marriage could be deduced e.g. "My fiancé" or "My future wife".

By using express words at the end of each and every clause in the will indicating that it was in contemplation of marriage.

---

(1)Re. Hodgkinson (1893) P.339

(2)Re. Durance (1872) LR 2 P & D 406

(3)Re. Robinson (1930) 2 CH 332

(4)Re. Phelan (1971) 3 All ER 1256

(5)Re. Everest (Dec'd) (1975) 1 All ER 672

(6)Clarke V Scipps (1852) 2 RUB. ECC 562

(7)Cheese V Lovejoy (1877) 1 P & D 251

(8)Re. Nunn (1936) 1 All E.R 555

(9)Re. Booth (1926)P. 118

(10) Gill V Gill (1909) P.157

(11) Re. Dadds (1857) Dea & SW 290

(12) Dixon V Treasury Solicitor (1905) P. 42

(13) Re. Jones (1976) 1 All ER 593

(14) Re. Southerden (1925)P. 177

(15) Re. Roberts (Dec'd) (1970) 3 All ER 225

Re. Davey (Dec'd) (1980) 3 All ER 342

(16) Coleman (1975) All 675

CHAPTER 25

ALTERATION, REVIVAL, ORAL WILLS

ALTERATION

No erasure, writing, in between lines or other alteration made in a written will after it has been signed in the usual manner, shall have any effect unless the alteration is signed and attested in the same way as a written will is required to be done.

For the alteration to be valid, the signature of the testator and witnesses should be made in the margin or on some other part of the will opposite or near to the alteration. It can also be referred to in a memorandum written at the end or some other part of the will and so signed and attested.

Where, on the other hand if a typewritten or printed will needs to be completed by the filling in of any blank spaces, there shall be a presumption that the will has been duly executed. (2)

REVIVAL

No will which has been made in any manner wholly revoked shall be revived otherwise than by signing and attesting, again, in the usual manner. (3)

Where only part of the will has been revoked, that part shall _not_ be revived otherwise, than by re-execution thereof in the usual manner. One can also have a subsequent will or codicil showing an intention to revive it. (4)

ORAL WILLS

A will may be made either orally or in writing.

An oral will is only valid if made before two or more competent witnesses, and if T (T = Testator) dies within a period of three months from the date of making the will.

If an oral will is contrary to any written will, whether it was made before or after the oral will, the written will has precedence in so far as it is contrary to the oral will.

An oral will made by a member of the armed forces or merchant marine during a period of active service, shall be valid if the testator dies during the period of active service, notwithstanding the fact that he dies more than 3 months after the date of making the will." Therefore his oral will is valid even if made more than 3 months before his death but he must have been in "active service" when he dies.

The main reason for privilege is the person to whom it is accorded i.e. soldiers and sailors when in active service can be placed in danger and therefore unable to obtain proper legal advice on making a will. (i)

There are several reported cases on the issue of what is "active service". In a modern case, (ii). The deceased case was a soldier serving in Northern Ireland.

While on a military patrol intended to assist in the maintenance of law and order, he was shot and wounded by a known gunman. On the way to hospital the deceased said to the officers, "If I don't make it, make sure Anne gets all my stuff." This was held to be a valid will even though the enemy was un-uniformed of band of assassins and arsonists.

The privilege was not, however, allowed to an apprentice to a shipping company at home between voyages. (iii)

In another case, (iv) the deceased only had orders to sail at the time she made the alleged will in the form of a letter to a friend. The orders to sail were considered sufficient and entitled her to make a privileged will even though she was on dry land when she made it.

One must have testamentary intent (v) thus in a decided case the court refused to treat the words spoken by a barmaid on a liner to a fellow barman in a casual conversation, as valid.

It was held (vi) that although the words must be spoken or written with testamentary intent, the deceased need not be aware that he is making a will e.g. "If I stop a bullet, everything of mine will be yours" or "If I don't make it make sure Anne gets all my stuff". (vii)

---

(1)   Re. Wingham (1949) P.187

(2)   Re. Jones (1981) 1 All ER 1

(3)   Re. Rapleys Estate (1983) 3 All Er 248

(4)   Re. Hales Goods (1915) 2 IR 362

(5)   In the estate of Knibbs (1962) 1 WLR 852

(6)   Re. Stable (Dec'd) (1919)P.7

(7)   Re. Jones (Dec'd) (1987) 1 All ER

CHAPTER 26

CAN A TESTATOR OR TESTATRIX DISINHERIT A DEPENDANT?

If the court, on the application by or on behalf of a dependant, finds that reasonable provision has not been made for this dependant, it can order that such reasonable provision as thinks fit, shall be made for that dependent out of the deceased's net estate (whether the deceased died testate (having made a will) or wholly or partly intestate (having made no will or having made a will but not dealt with certain assets therein (1).

The court may only order provision to be made for an applicant if the court is satisfied that the disposition of the deceased's estate is not such as to make reasonable financial provision for the applicant. (2)

In making provision for a dependent the court shall have complete discretion to order a specific share of the estate to be given to the dependant or to order periodic payments "and to impose such conditions as it thinks fit". (3)

In a decided case [4] the court ordered the transfer to a dependant specified property comprised in the deceased's net estate.

In considering whether any order should be made the court shall have regard to:

The nature and amount of the deceased's property;

Any past, present and future capital or income from any source;

The existing and future means and needs of the dependent

Whether the deceased had made any inter vivos gift (gift during the deceased lifetime) to the dependent)

The conduct of the dependant in relation to the deceased

The situation and circumstances of the deceased's other dependants and beneficiaries under any will

The general circumstances of the case, including the deceased's reasons for not making any provision for the dependant in his or her will. [5]

UK statutory law does not specifically allow for "former wife or wives" but case law does allow for certain classes of former spouses. Subsequent case law also provides for polygamous marriages.

In a decided case (7) a generous approach was made to a claim by adult children. An adult son took half of Ts 13000 pound estate under Ts will.

It was held that this was not a reasonable provision and Ts 9000 pound house was ordered transferred to the son.

This case was criticized because there was no evidence that the son was in any need.

How does one define "Maintenance"?

The facts of a recent case (8) were that the deceased and applicant lived together from 1949 until the deceased's death in 1976, in a bungalow owned by the deceased. When they retired, each received a state pension. The applicant paid the deceased for his accommodation and contributed to the weekly shopping bill.

The deceased paid all the outgoings on the bungalow and did housework and cooking. The applicant owned and maintained a car for their joint use and also did gardening and decorating work around the bungalow for which he was reimbursed by the deceased. Before her death the deceased gave the applicant 550 pounds of premium bonds and by her will left

204

her bungalow to her three sisters. The applicant claimed and the question which arose was whether the applicant was being "maintained".

It was held that the applicant was one of the two people of independent means who had chosen to pool their individual resources to enable them to live together without either undertaking any responsibility for maintaining the other—the claim therefore failed, as she was not mentioned.

In another case (9) the applicant lived with the deceased from 1971, until the deceased's death 1979. Both were pensioners. The deceased was the widow of the applicant's brother-in-law who lived alone in a house left to her in her late husband's will and she asked the applicant to live with her as she was lonely and frightened. The applicant agreed to share the house and to pool their income to meet living expenses.

The applicant provided some furniture, tended the garden and carried out some household jobs. The deceased provided the applicant with rent free accommodation and did all his cooking and washing. When the deceased died in 1979 she left her estate including the house to her children and made no provision for the applicant who applied for reasonable financial provision.

It was held that the free accommodation was a significant contribution to the reasonable needs, especially of an old age pensioner and it was provided for eight years and this amounted to the assumption of the responsibility of the applicant's maintenance.

Therefore it was held that unless the applicants' contributions equaled or outweighed the benefit of rent free accommodation he would be treated as a "dependent" because the latter was being "maintained" and therefore could receive something from deceased's estate.

In a recent case [10], it was held that the flow of benefits between a couple living together were broadly commensurate and that would demonstrate the mutuality or their relationship this was the case, even though care and support was given to another during the last few years of someone's life.

The act does not make "anti-avoidance" provisions.

"Avoidance" can take place where the deceased reduces the value of his net estate at his death so that no "dependent" can claim.

This can be done by reducing the property of which he had power to dispose of by his will or by increasing the debts and liabilities payable out of his estate e.g. entering into contract under a seal with a "donee" to pay the donee at his own death a sum of money large enough to exhaust his assets.

He may also enter into a contract with the donee to leave by his will a particular asset. In such cases the donee's claim would have precedence over that of the "dependent".

No claim under this part can be made after a grant of representation has been confirmed.

What circumstances will persuade the courts to grant leave to apply out of time? In the UK the court has the jurisdiction to accept applications after the time limit but would refuse it if the delay was the fault of the applicants or if almost all the estate had been distributed.

In a case that was decided it was held that the law cannot move to perfect an incomplete gift. The transfer to the plaintiff was blocked and hence not completed.

Where the wrong statutory form was therefore used to apply for grant, there was no procedure for substitution with the proper form.

It was also held that a will is not absolute; the court can interfere and make provision for dependents.

---

(2) Rajabally V Rajabally (1987) 2 FLR 390

(4) Harrington V Gill (1983) 265

(7) Re. Christie (1979) 1 All ER 546

(8) Re. Beaumont (1980) 1 All ER 267

(9) Jelley V Liffe (1981) 2 All ER 26

(10) Bishop V Plumley (1991) 1 All ER 236

CHAPTER 27

LEGACIES AND DEVICES AND THEIR FAILURE

LEGACIES AND DEVICES

The assets which are subject to disposition in the will are those belonging to the testator at the date, of his or her death. These assets can include assets acquired after the date the will was executed e.g. 'A gift of all my coins to John' in a will made in 1992, would include coins acquired in 1994, before the testator's death.

A gift in the will of freehold land is called "devise"; a gift of personal and household effects (clothing, furniture, appliances, pictures, ornaments, food, drinks, utensils etc) is called a "bequest", or "legacy".

a. Special Legacies

This has been defined (1) as a testamentary gift of a particular part of the property of the testator, which identifies that part by a sufficient description, whether in specific or in general terms, and manifests an intention, that, that part shall be enjoyed or taken in the state and condition indicated by that description. It has also been called a "specific legacy". An example would be "my Peugeot car".

The particular thing must be part of the testators estate at his/her death and the gift must be described in such a way as to sever or distinguish it from the rest of the estate.

A gift of a particular thing, for instance shares of certain types, is not a specific legacy if there is nothing on the face of the will to indicate that the testator was referring to shares belonging to him, even though he may have in fact owned the shares mentioned.

A gift of part of a specified fund has been held to be specific. Also a gift of money "out of" specific money, or stock "out of" specific stock is specific or special.

A gift of the whole of the testator's personal estate may be specific.

b. General Legacies

This is a testamentary gift (given by will) of property described in general terms, to be provided out of the general estate of the testator. A general legacy is a gift which is not a bequest of any specific part of the testator's. In other words, it is a gift of property which is not distinguished from other property of the same type e.g. 100, 000/= or a car for James. The gift is therefore to be provided out of the testator's general estate.

The important thing about a general legacy is that it need not actually be part of the testator's estate.

Because of the doctrine of ademption, the court leans strongly in favour of general and not specific legacies. Thus the chances of it being saved are better because general legacies do not fail by ademption.

c. Demonstrative Legacy

This has been defined in the act (2) as a testamentary gift which by its nature is general but which manifests an intention that the gift shall be primarily satisfied out of a specified fund or a specified part of the property of the testator, but shall, upon failure of that fund or property to be met from the general estate.

An example would be $100, 000/= from my account in ABC Bank.

d. Pecuniary Legacy

A general legacy of money is usually called a pecuniary legacy.

e. Devises

The essential nature of any devise is that it deals solely with the real estate of the testator.

There are two types of device:-

A specific devise is a gift of real property under a will. The gift must be part of the testator's estate at his death and it must be described in such a way as to sever or distinguish it from the rest of the estate. Such a devise passes all the rights and obligations which the testator had in the property. E.g. my farm in Limuru.

Residuary devise—This is a gift of real property by description. Thus; a gift of "all my farms to X" or "all my real property to Y" are residuary devices.

f. Annuities

An annuity is, in general, a legacy of money payable by installments. There are three types:-

Specific (a gift of an already existing annuity)
General (to be paid out of the testators estate)

212

Demonstrative (to be paid primarily out of a specified fund or specific part of the testator's property).

How long will the annuity last?

This depends on the true construction of the will. If it is simply "to A" then it is for A's lifetime only. However, if the annuity is given to a corporation or an incorporated body capable of existing indefinitely then the annuity is on the face of it perpetual.

There is no interest payable in arrears of annuity, unless the non-payment of the annuity is the fault of those who hold the fund out of which it is to be paid.

THE DOCTRINE OF ADEMPTION

A special or specific legacy (particular part of the testator's property) (a), above specific devise (gift of real estate e (i) above or specific annuity (f) (i) above (gift of an already existing annuity) all fail by ademption if, at the testators death, the subject matter for the gift has been destroyed or converted into something else by an act of the testator.

A legacy of specific chattels (e.g. personal property) is <u>adeemed</u> if they are sold during the testators lifetime, or if they lost or destroyed during or at the testators death.

As a general rule, even if the chattels are insured, the beneficiary has no right to the insurance monies. The same applies to a specific piece of land which is afterwards sold.

If the testator sells stocks and shares, the gift will <u>adeem,</u> and the fact that the testator may subsequently purchase replacement securities will not revive the gift, since this will not be the specific gift.

Where there has been a change in name and form only of shares etc there is no ademption.

Where a testator makes a specific bequest of debt owed to him, it will adeem if the debt subsequently gets paid.

ADEMPTION BY CONTRACT

A contract of sale entered by the testator after the date of the will, though not completed until after the testators death, will cause the gift to adeem. The beneficiary is, however, entitled to enjoy the property until the completion of the sale.

If, however, the testator makes a binding contract for sale, giving the property away, before making the will, then the beneficiary is entitled to the proceeds of sale.

ADEMPTION BY EXERCISE OF AN OPTION TO PURCHASE

Where a beneficiary is entitled to a specific gift of property which later becomes the subject of an option to purchase granted by the testator to a third party, the beneficiary is entitled to nothing, even if the third party does not exercise the option after the testator's death.

This is known as the rule in Lawes V Bennett.

However, if the option has been arranged before the making of the gift, the beneficiary is entitled to the price payable under the option.

The date from which the will speaks

Specific gifts which speak as from the death do not strictly a deem. Thus a gift to X of "the car which I own at my death" does not fail by ademption even though the testator may have changed his car since the date of the will.

The gift is to be ascertained at the testator's death and not at the date of the will and can therefore only fail if there is no car owned by the testator at his death.

Demonstrative and general legacies and annuities are not subject to ademption, since they are to be provided out of the general estate.

The doctrine of Lapse

A devise or legacy lapses if the beneficiary predeceases (dies before) the testator. The burden of proving that a beneficiary has survived the testator shall lie on the person alleging survivorship (3). This is subject to the presumption of survivorship contained in the act (4).

According to this doctrine, where two or more persons have died in circumstances rendering in uncertain which of them survived the other or others, the death shall, for the purpose of this act, be presumed to have occurred in order of seniority; accordingly the younger shall be deemed to have survived the elder. On the other hand, in the case of spouses who died in those circumstances, the spouses shall be presumed to have died simultaneously.

Exceptions to the doctrine of lapse

Unless a contrary intention appears in the will, there shall be no lapse in either of the following cases:-

  Where the gift or disposition is made in discharge of a moral obligation recognized by the testator.

  Where the gift is in favour of any child or other issue of the testator and the said child or issue as the case may be, leaves issue.

(A person's issue comprises his children, grandchildren or other lineal descendants.)

In either of the above cases, the gift or disposition shall take effect as if the deceased beneficiary died immediately after the testator, and so the gift foes to the issue of the deceased's beneficiary.

Re. Hodgkinson (1893) P.339

Re. Durance (1872) LR 2 P & D 406

Re. Robinson (1930) 2 CH 332

Re. Phelan (1971) 3 All ER 1256

Re. Everest (Dec'd) (1975) 1 All ER 672

Clarke V Scipps (1852) 2 RUB. ECC 562

Cheese V Lovejoy (1877) 1 P & D 251

Re. Nunn (1936) 1 All E.R 555

Re. Booth (1926)P. 118

(10) Gill V Gill (1909) P.157

(11) Re. Dadds (1857) Dea & SW 290

(12) Dixon V Treasury Solicitor (1905) P. 42

(13) Re. Jones (1976) 1 All ER 593

(14) Re. Southerden (1925)P. 177

(15) Re. Roberts (Dec'd) (1970) 3 All ER 225

Re. Davey (Dec'd) (1980) 3 All ER 342

(16) Coleman (1975) All 675

CHAPTER 28

INTESTACY

Intestacy is either total or partial. There is a total intestacy where the deceased does not effectively dispose of any of his or her property in his will. There is a partial intestacy where the deceased effectively disposes of some, but not all of his or her property by will.

If none can be found to survive the intestate, the net intestate estate devolves upon the state, and be paid into the consolidated fund.

Firstly, what are "personal and household effects" that the spouse gets from the intestate? (5). This does not include things used for the business of the intestate.

The value of an item is immaterial in deciding whether it falls under the above definition. In a decided case (6), a collection of clocks and watches valued 50,000 pounds was held to be a personal chattel.

It does not also appear relevant that the deceased had a collection of certain items as

investment. In another case (7) it was held that
a stamp collection value 1,848 pounds as an
investment was a personal chattel.

The definition includes almost all items which
might be found in the home of the average
citizen and so chattels (movable possessions which
were used by the deceased for business purposes)
are excluded from the definition and partial
usage for business purposes is sufficient to exclude
it as a personal effect. (8).

Money and securities for money are also excluded
but notes and coins kept as a collection would be
a personal effect.

Secondly, where the intestate has left no surviving
spouse or children, what would be the effect of
one class of relatives disclaiming their intestate
entitlement? (9)

In a decided case (10) T, who died in 1973 left a
will dated 1964 by which she left her residuary
(the rest of her) estate for her sister and brother
during their joint lives and then to the survivor
of the said brother and after the death of the
survivor for all, or any of the children of her
brother who shall be living at T's death or born
thereafter. There was an ultimate gift to a charity.

At T's death, the brother was 78 and the sister 82 and neither had children. The brother and sister disclaimed their interest in the residuary estate. The question was whether there was "acceleration" so that the charity took the gift. It was held that because it was still possible that the brother might have children, the doctrine of acceleration was excluded and charity was excluded. Where an intestate has married more than once (under any system of law permitting polygamy), the intestate personal and household effects and the residue of the net intestate estate shall, in the first instance, be divided among the houses according to the number of the children in each house but also adding any wife surviving him as an additional unit to the number of children. (11) If a man became a polygamist in the UK and UK law does not allow polygamy then this section would not apply, and the other wives would not get anything. If a child who receives according to the above rules is a minor, such assets shall be held in trusts until such time as the minor attains 18 years or, if a female, marries under that age. (12) If the said child X does not attain 18 and has children, Y & Z, and X dies, the share that X would have got is shared between Y & Z in the same way.

Previous benefits (advancement) are to be brought into account in determining the share of the net intestate estate finally accruing to the said child or grandchild.

What is advancement? A decided case [13] contains some discussion on what constitutes a contrary intention for the purpose of this section. A father who owned a family company gave each of his 3 children 600 shares in the company. One daughter X subsequently married a man who the father strongly disapproved of. On his death the father left the whole of his estate to his wife, including the remaining shareholding in the company. The widow gave all the remaining shares in the company to the other two children in her lifetime and eventually died intestate. X claimed that the lifetime gift of shares to the other two children should be taken in account as an advancement, thereby reducing their entitlement on a distribution of the assets of the intestate.

It was held that the widow had shown an intention not to give X any further shares but it could not be concluded from that, that she also intended to exclude X from her inheritance altogether because she had not directed her mind as to what should happen to her property on her death.

222

---

6. Re. Crispins Will Trusts (1975) 1 Ch. 245

7. Re. Reynolds Will Trusts (1966) 1 WLR 19

8. Collins WT (1971) 1 WLR 37

10. Re. Scott (Dec'd) (1975) 2 All ER 10

13. Hardy V. Shaw (1926) 1 CH. 82

CHAPTER 29

A SAMPLE WILL

LAST WILL AND TESTAMENT
OF

I, _____ being of sound mind and under no restraint, hereby publish and declare this instrument to be my Last Will and Testament, revoking all previous Wills and Codicils I have made.

1. I am married to, _____ of the same address. I have no children.
2. I give the entire residue of my estate, whether real, personal or mixed, to my aforementioned husband.

In the event that my husband predeceases me I give the entire residue of my estate to;

50% to _____
50% to _____

3. I nominate and appoint my husband as Executor of this, my Last Will and Testament. If the above-named Executor is unable or

unwilling to serve, or _____, Trust Corporation of Canada.

4. I direct my Executor to pay all of my legally enforceable debts, the expenses of my funeral and burial, and the expenses of the administration of my estate out of my residuary estate.

5. In the event that Trust Corporation is appointed as Co—Executor and Trustee I declare that the said Trust Corporation of Canada shall be entitled to receive and shall be paid out of my estate, or any trust established by my will as the case may be, as compensation for its acting as an executor and/or trustee of and under this my will, the fees, reimbursement and other compensation provided for in the Compensation Agreement between the Trust Corporation of Canada and myself, signed on the ___ day of 20 ___ prior to the execution of this my Will, and I declare that the terms of the said Compensation Agreement shall be valid and binding in all respects to fix the compensation payable to Trust Corporation of Canada as though the Compensation Agreement was expressly embodied in this my Will.

Deposit of Assets

6. My trustees may deposit estate and trust assets in a financial institution in which

my trustees or an agent of or advisor to my trustees have an interest, notwithstanding that my trustees and or my Trustees' agent or advisor may benefit there from, and my Trustees shall not be required to account for, or to give up, any such benefit. In particular, it shall not be improper for my Trustees to deposit moneys of my estate or any trust created by my will in Trust or its affiliated, subsidiary, holding or related Companies

7. In addition to the foregoing powers and those conferred to my Executor by law, I authorize my Executor to do all acts which my Executor deems necessary and/or appropriate in order to achieve the purposes of this, my Last Will and Testament, including the power to sell or dispose of property and distribute the proceeds of such sale or disposal as part of my estate; to retain property without liability for any depreciation or loss which may result; to settle, compromise, or abandon any claim either for or against my estate; to vote stock or exercise any of the rights of ownership of any stocks or bonds which form a part of this estate; to continue or participate in the operations of any business which forms a part of this estate, all as fully as I could do if living.

8. My husband and I have insurance policies with such policies contain details of beneficiaries.

9. I authorize my Executor to utilize the services of an attorney, accountant and any other professional as may be necessary or desirable in the administration of this, my Last Will and Testament. The expenses incurred by my Executor using such professional services shall be an expense to my estate and shall be paid by my estate.

10. I direct my Executor to pay out of the assets of my residuary estate, all inheritance, transfer, estate and similar taxes (including interest and penalties) on any property or interest in property included in my estate for the purpose of computing taxes.

11. It is not my intention to make provisions in this, my Last Will and Testament, for any relative or any other person not expressly provided for herein, and if any such person has not been expressly mentioned herein, he or she has been omitted by myself intentionally and with full knowledge of his or her relationship and existence, and not by any oversight or neglect.

12. Where appropriate to the context, pronouns or other terms expressed in one number or gender shall be deemed to include the other number or gender, as the case may be. The word executor shall be deemed to include Trustee

13. Any person or organization named or referred to herein shall be deemed to have survived me only if such person or

organization shall in fact survive me for a period of at least thirty (30) days. Any person or organization named or referred to herein who shall not survive me for a period of at least thirty (30) days shall be deemed to have died before I do.

14. With regard to burial instructions, It is my desire that my remains be cremated in accordance with specific instructions left with the

IN WITNESS WHEREOF, I have signed my name, declaring and publishing this instrument as my Last Will and Testament, in the presence of the undersigned Witnesses on this _____ day of _____, 20___.

ATTESTATION

We hereby certify that this Last Will and Testament was signed, declared and published as her Last Will and Testament on this _____ day of _____, 20 in our presence and in the presence of each other, and we sign our names below as Witnesses in her presence, at her request and in the presence of each other on this _____ day of _____, 20___.

_____ Resides at _____

Witness (1) Signature   Street Address

_____   _____
Witness (1) Name   *(Printed) City, Province*

_____ *Resides at* _____
Witness (2) Signature   *Street Address*

_____   _____
Witness (2) Name   *(Printed) City, Province*

AFFIDAVIT

We, _____, _____,
and _____, the Testator and
Witnesses, having first been duly sworn, do
solemnly swear that in our presence and in
the presence of each other, signed, declared
and published the foregoing instrument on
the____day of_____, 20   , as her Last
Will and Testament, and asked each of us to serve
as Witnesses. Each of the Witnesses signed this Last
Will and Testament as Witnesses, in the presence
of and in the presence of each other. At the time
of signing this Last Will and Testament, appeared
to us to be of sound mind, free from duress, fraud
or undue influence. Each of us who signed
the foregoing instrument as a Witness is fully
competent to serve as a Witness.

_____   _____
Date   Testator

_____   _____
Date   Witness (1)

_____   _____
Date   Witness (2)

*Subscribed and sworn to before me
by _____, _____,
and _____, each of whom is
known to me personally, this_____ day
of _____, 20____.*

Personal Care Directive

This is the Advance directive of _____ *of*

Appointment of Agent

1. *I appoint my* <u>wife</u> _____ *, based in* _____ *, failing which, my off springs,* _____ *currently based in* _____ *and, also based in* _____ *or the survivors thereof, jointly, to make personal and health care decisions on my behalf when I am no longer able to make or communicate my own health or personal care decisions due to lack of capacity.*

Duty to Consult

Before making any decisions about my health or personal care my agents must try to discuss it with me, even if the declarations above have been completed.

<u>*Basis for making decisions.*</u>

If I am unable to communicate:

I give my agent power to make decisions about the following personal and health care matters:

To consent, refuse or withdraw consent to any type of health care.

232

To authorize my admission to or discharge from any medical care facility.

I do not want my life prolonged if treatments will leave me in a condition of permanent unconsciousness.

Resolution of disputes

If any dispute arises about the interpretation about my wishes about the validity of this directive or about any related matter I encourage my agent to pursue alternate dispute resolution systems.

SIGNED, SEALED, and DELIVERED.

Signature

_____

_____

Signature of witness

_____

Name of witness

_____

Address

Signature of witness

Name of witness

Personal Care Directive

This is the Advance directive of

Currently residing at;

Appointment of Agent

I appoint my wife/son/daughter,   , based in   , to make personal and health care decisions on my behalf when I am no longer able to make or communicate my own health or personal care decisions due to lack of capacity.

Duty to Consult

Before making any decisions about my health or personal care my agents must try to discuss it with me, even if the declarations above have been completed.

Basis for making decisions.

If I am unable to communicate:

I give my agent power to make decisions about the following personal and health care matters:

To consent, refuse or withdraw consent to any type of health care.

To authorize my admission to or discharge from any medical care facility

I do not want my life prolonged if treatments will leave me in a condition of permanent unconsciousness

Resolution of disputes

If any dispute arises about the interpretation about my wishes about the validity of this directive or about any related matter I encourage my agent to pursue alternate dispute resolution systems.

SIGNED, SEALED, and DELIVERED.

Signature

_____

_____

Signature of witness

_____

Name of witness

_____

Address

_____

Signature of witness

_____

Name of witness

_____

Address

POWER OF ATTORNEY

This POWER OF ATTORNEY is given on the _____ day of _____, 20__

by

of

I appoint my husband to be my true and lawful attorney, for me and in my name and for my sole use and benefit to do on my behalf anything that I can otherwise lawfully do by an attorney.

In the event that my said husband fails to survive me I appoint to act, jointly with Trust Corporation of Canada, with the following powers:

   i) In its discretion, to deposit any or all of my assets in a financial institution in which Trust, its affiliated, subsidiary, holding or related companies or its agent or advisor may have an interest (called collectively the Financial Group"), notwithstanding that

Trust or the Financial Group may benefit therefrom,

   ii) To manage my financial affairs by opening and/or continuing to operate one or more custodial, non-discretionary managed or discretionary managed accounts at The

Trust and/or with Private Counsel Inc. or another Financial Group member company, or such account(s) with other financial institutions whether or not a member of the Financial Group, as it from time to time deems advisable (the "Account" or "Accounts"), and to transfer or deposit Any or all of my assets into such Account or Any Account or Accounts to be held in my name or the name of its agents or nominees, and to sell or dispose of Any or all of my assets and deposit the net sale proceeds into such Account or Accounts, without being required to diversify my assets; and to charge the fees in effect from time to time for such Account or Accounts to the assets in the Account or Accounts, and which fees are not to be considered in determining the compensation Royal Trust may otherwise receive for acting as my attorney but are to be in addition thereto; and

iii) In its discretion, to invest and reinvest at Any time and from time to time all or any of my assets in any investment, whether or not income producing, including:

Where appropriate to the context, pronouns or other terms expressed in one number or gender shall be deemed to include the other number or gender, as the case may be.

I declare that, after due consideration, I am satisfied that the authority conferred on the attorney named in this power of attorney is adequate to provide the competent and effectual management of all my estate in case I should become a patient in a psychiatric facility and be certified as not competent to manage my estate under the Mental Health Act I agree for myself, my heirs, executors, and administrators, to ratify and confirm all that my said attorney(s) shall do or cause to be done by virtue of this power of attorney.

_____

Date

Witness (1)

_____

Date

Witness (2)

Subscribed and sworn to before me
by _____, _____, and _____,
each of whom is known to me personally, this
_____ day of _____, 20____.

SIGNED, SEALED, and DELIVERED.

240

Signature

_____

_____

Signature of witness

_____

Name of witness

_____

Address

_____

Signature of witness

_____

Name of witness

_____

Address

LAST WILL AND TESTAMENT
OF

I,   , of   , being of sound
mind and under no restraint, hereby publish
and declare this instrument to be my Last Will
and Testament, revoking all previous Wills and
Codicils I have made.

1. I am married to of the same address. I have
   no children.
2. I give the entire residue of my estate,
   whether real, personal or mixed, to my
   aforementioned wife.

In the event that my wife predeceases me I give
the entire residue of my estate to the following;

      50% to
      50% to

3. I nominate and appoint my wife, as
   the Executor of this, my Last Will and
   Testament. If the above-named Executor is
   unable or unwilling to serve, or otherwise
   fails to complete the Administration of my
   estate, I appoint to serve instead, with Trust
   Corporation of as co-executor.
4. I direct my Executor to pay all of my legally
   enforceable debts, the expenses of my funeral
   and burial, (unless the pre-arranged

payment has been made in full already) and the expenses of the administration of my estate out of my residuary estate.

5. In the event that Trust Corporation is appointed as Co-Executor and Trustee I declare that the said Royal Trust Corporation of Canada shall be entitled to receive and shall be paid out of my estate, or any trust established by my will as the case may be, as compensation for its acting as the Co Executor and/or trustee of and under this my will, the fees, reimbursement and other compensation provided for in the Compensation Agreement between the Trust Corporation of Canada and myself, signed on the _____ day of _____ 20 prior to the execution of this my Will, and I declare that the terms of the said Compensation Agreement shall be valid and binding in all respects to fix the compensation payable to l Trust Corporation of Canada as though the Compensation Agreement was expressly embodied in this my Will.

Deposit of Assets

6. My Trustees may deposit estate and trust assets in a financial institution in which my trustees or an agent of or advisor to my Trustees have an interest, notwithstanding that my Trustees and or my Trustees' agent or advisor may benefit there from, and my

Trustees shall not be required to account for, or to give up, any such benefit. In particular, it shall not be improper for my Trustees to deposit moneys of my estate or any trust created by my will in Trust or its affiliated, subsidiary, holding or related companies

7. In addition to the powers conferred to my Executor by law, I authorize my Executor to do all acts which my Executor deems necessary and/or appropriate in order to achieve the purposes of this, my Last Will and Testament, including the power to sell or dispose of property and distribute the proceeds of such sale or disposal as part of my estate; to retain property without liability for any depreciation or loss which may result; to settle, compromise, or abandon any claim either for or against my estate; to vote stock or exercise any of the rights of ownership of any stocks or bonds which form a part of this estate; to continue or participate in the operations of any business which forms a part of this estate, all as fully as I could do if living.

8. My wife and I have insurance policies with Such policies contain details of beneficiaries.

9. I authorize my Executor to utilize the services of an attorney, accountant and any other professional as may be necessary or desirable in the administration of this, my Last Will and Testament. The expenses incurred by my Executor using such professional services

244

shall be an expense to my estate and shall be paid by my estate.

10. I direct my Executor to pay out of the assets of my residuary estate, all inheritance, transfer, estate and similar taxes (including interest and penalties) on any property or interest in property included in my estate for the purpose of computing taxes.

11. It is not my intention to make provisions in this, my Last Will and Testament, for any relative or any other person not expressly provided for herein, and if any such person has not been expressly mentioned herein, he or she has been omitted by myself intentionally and with full knowledge of his or her relationship and existence, and not by any oversight or neglect.

12. Where appropriate to the context, pronouns or other terms expressed in one number or gender shall be deemed to include the other number or gender, as the case may be. The word executor shall be deemed to include Trustee

13. Any person or organization named or referred to herein shall be deemed to have survived me only if such person or organization shall in fact survive me for a period of at least thirty (30) days. Any person or organization named or referred to herein who shall not survive me for a period of at least thirty (30) days shall be deemed to have died before I do.

14. With regard to burial instructions, It is my desire that my remains be cremated in accordance with specific instructions left with the

15. IN WITNESS WHEREOF, I have signed my name, declaring and publishing this instrument as my Last Will and Testament, in the presence of the undersigned Witnesses on this _____ day of _____, 20____ .

ATTESTATION

We hereby certify that this Last Will and Testament was signed, declared and published as his Last Will and Testament on this _____ day of _____, 20 in our presence and in the presence of each other, and we sign our names below as Witnesses in his presence, at her request and in the presence of each other on this _____ day of _____, 20____ .

_____ Resides at _____
Witness (1) Signature   Street Address

_____   _____
Witness (1) Name   (Printed) City, Province

_____ Resides at _____
Witness (2) Signature   Street Address

_____   _____
Witness (2) Name   (Printed) City, Province

AFFIDAVIT

We, _____,_____,
and _____, the Testator
and Witnesses, having first been duly sworn,
do solemnly swear that in our presence and
in the presence of each other, signed, declared
and published the foregoing instrument on
the ___ day of _____, 20___, as his Last
Will and Testament, and asked each of us to serve
as Witnesses. Each of the Witnesses signed this Last
Will and Testament as Witnesses, in the presence
of and in the presence of each other. At the time
of signing this Last Will and Testament, appeared
to us to be of sound mind, free from duress, fraud
or undue influence. Each of us who signed
the foregoing instrument as a Witness is fully
competent to serve as a Witness.

_____   _____
Date   Testator

_____   _____
Date   Witness (1)

_____   _____
Date   Witness (2)

Subscribed and sworn to before me
by _____, _____,
and _____, each of
whom is known to me personally, this _____
day of _____

CHAPTER 30

GLOSSARY OF TERMS

[COMPLILED FROM OSBORNS CONCISE LAW DICTIONARY 7ᵀᴴ EDITION BY ROGER BIRD, PUBLISHED BY SWEET & MAXWELL]

ADEMPTION—A specific legacy is said to be adeemed when, as a result of implied revocation by a testator is withheld or extinguished e.g. if he makes a gift "if my gold ring" and sells it before his death.

ADMINISTRATION—Process of collecting the assets of a deceased person, paying debts and distributing any surplus to those entitled.

ADMINISTER—To collect the assets, pay all debts owned from the estate and distribute the rest to the beneficiaries.

ASSENT—The instrument or act whereby a personal representation effects a disposition in a will by transferring it to the person entitled to it.

ASSETS—physical property or rights which have a value in monetary terms.

ATTESTATION—The signature of a document by one who is not a party to it, but who is the witness to the signature of another.

AVOIDANCE—Setting aside, making null and void.

BENEFICIARY—A person or organization which receives a gift from the estate.

BEQUEST—A gift, sometimes called a benefit.

CHATTELS—Generally property other than freehold land e.g. personal property

CODICIL—An addition or supplement to a will after the finishing of it. It must be executed with all the formalities appropriate to the execution of a will.

DEPENDENT RELATIVE REVOCATION—Where the revocation of a will is relative to another will and is intended to be dependent upon the fact that the other will being valid, then unless that other will take effect, the revocation is ineffective.

DEVISE—A gift of real property by will.

DEVOLUTION—The passing of property or right from one person to another e.g. on death.

DONATIO MORTIS CAUSA—A gift of property by a donor in anticipation of his death.

ESTATE (NET)—In relation to a deceased person, it includes property which he had power to dispose of by will, less funeral, testamentary and administration expenses.

ESTATE (Administration of)—Procedure relating to assets of deceased person, whereby they are collected, debts are paid and the surplus distributed to those beneficially entitled.

ESTATE—The total assets you own when you die.

EXECUTE—To carry out the legal procedure to make a will valid under the law.

EXECUTOR—A person you chose to administer your estate.

GENERAL LEGACY—A bequest which does not identify specifically the thing bequeathed. The subject matter of a general legacy need not form part of the testator's assets at the time of his death.

HOLOGRAM—A will written in the testator's own handwriting.

HOTCHSPOT—The bringing together of properties into a common lot so that equality of division may be assured

INTER VIVOS—A transaction between living persons.

INTESTACY (partial)—This results from a will which disposes of only part of the deceased property.

JOINT WILL—One document in which two or more persons incorporate their testamentary wishes.

LAPSE—Failure of a legacy or devise because of the death of the beneficiary before that of the testator.

LEGACY—A gift of personal property by will; a gift of money.

MAINTENANCE—The supply of necessaries e.g. food, clothing.

MUTUAL WILLS—Wills made by two or more persons, conferring reciprocal benefits, or based on an agreement to make such wills an not revoke them without the consent of the other.

THE RULE AGAINST PERPETUITIES—Where there is a possibility that a future interest in property might vest after expiration of the perpetuity period, such as interest is generally void.

PERSONAL REPRESENTATIVE—The executor of administer of the deceased person.

PROBATE—Document issued under the seal of the court as official evidence of the authority of an executor.

Legal proof that a will is valid, giving authority to administer.

RESIDUE—The remainder of the estate after debts, legacies, funeral and other expenses have been taken off.

REVOKE—To legally cancel.

REVOCATION OF WILL—A will can always be revoked by the testator before his death. This can be destruction of the will or by the execution of another will or codicil or as a result of marriage.

SPECIFIC LEGACY—A gift of a particular property e.g. a house, a car or a piece of furniture.

SPOUSE—The person to whom you are married.

SURVIVE—To be alive after the death of the will-maker.

TESTATOR—A man who makes a will.

TESTATRIX—A female testator.

TESTATE—Having made and left ones will.

TESTAMENT—A will.

TRUST—A legal arrangement to hold property for someone else—usually a child.

In essence, an equitable obligation, imposing on a person (trustee) certain duties of dealing with property held by him for the benefit of beneficiaries.

WILL—A revocable declaration made in the prescribed form, of the intentions of the maker concerning the disposition and devolution of ones property and other matters, which ones desires should become effective on and after his death.

CHAPTER 31

THE INTERNATIONAL SCENE

Canada

Rules are generally similar to that referred to in this book albeit with certain differences. The right to make a will can be available which a person reaches the age of 18 or 19, depending on the province,

Holograph wills are allowed i.e where a document purporting to be a will is handwritten by the testator and signed at the end.

A divorce will not revoke a will but in Alberta, New Brunswick, Nova Scotia and Newfoundland, after divorce a spouse is deemed to have predeceased the testator on the appointment of a Personal representative or the bequest of any or part of an estate.

Each province has legislation on dependent relief whilst intestacy rules are similar across Canada. Claims can be barred if made 6 months or more after death or probate, depending on each province.

Canada as well as The USA provides for dower rights where restrictions are placed on the ability of a married person to transfer property during the lifetime and at the death of this person.

<u>Property estate and probate</u>

Under the Canadian constitution, the law concerning property and therefore estate and probate matters lies within provincial jurisdiction. All common law jurisdictions in Canada have enacted legislation in relation to property, probate of wills and administration and deceased's estates.

Probate practice predominately depends upon court rules of practice in the superior court system of the particular province and territory.

Intro: Although the provinces have similar rules, there are differences. No province has forced heirship laws. Most provinces specifically recognize rights of common law and same sex couples for purposes of entitlement under dependant relief, family law and/or intestacy legislation. Entitlements and rules differ for each province.

256

Wills:

The requirements for a valid will are set out in legislation. Generally, a will must be made by a component adult (over the age of 18 or 19). The test for capacity follows 19th century English case law. All provinces except British Columbia and Prince Edward Island recognize holograph wills even so these provinces recognize holograph wills prepared by someone in a jurisdiction where holograph wills are recognized or where the jurisdiction is the testators domicile. In these provinces a holograph will is not valid to transfer real property interests situated within the province.

There are four types of wills recognized in Canada. The most common is the conventional will signed at its end by the tester in the presence of two witnesses who also sign, Holograph wills are the handwriting of the testator. In Québec, although conventional wills and holograph wills are in recognized the most common will is a notarial will signed by the testator and witnessed by the notary and one other witness the notary holds the original copy of the will notaries copies of which are deemed to be originals. A notarial will does not need to be probated in Quebec and usually does not need to be probated in other Canadian jurisdictions. The fourth is the international will. The provinces of Alberta, Manitoba, Ontario, New Brunswick, Newfoundland, Nova Scotia, Prince Edward Island and Saskatchewan have all signed the international convention.

A will may be revoked by making a new will that revokes all previous wills, or by destruction. If two wills are prepared to deal with different assets or assets in other jurisdictions, one will must not revoke the other. Changes to a will may be made at a later date with a codicil that must be prepared in accordance with the rules for making a will. Marriage revokes all wills/, unless the will was specifically made in contemplation of marriage. Quebec does not have this rule. New Brunswick Ontario and Nova Scotia have rules that may save a will prepared prior to marriage.

When the beneficiary has predeceased the testator, the gift lapses unless there is contrary intention in the will. Legacies to these beneficiaries fall into residue. If the beneficiary was to share in the residue, then that share of the residue is distributed as if there were intestacy, again subject to contrary intention in the will.

Gifts to a class of beneficiaries are distributed to the remainder of that class, subject to statutory anti-lapse rules. Gifts to two or more persons as joint tenants with the right of survivorship are

258

distributed to the survivors, as tenants in common are subject to the lapse rules, above.

Dependents relief

Each province has legislation permitting dependants to apply for support from the estate if they do not believe that the will or the devolution on intestacy makes adequate provision for them. The dependants relief rules in British Columbia and Nova Scotia apply only to devolution by will with no remedies under intestacy.

Intestacy rules

Intestacy rules are similar across Canada. The spouse is entitled to a specified amount and the residue is divided between the spouse and children. If an individual dies without a will leaving only a spouse, the spouse usually takes the entire estate. If there is no spouse, the children share equally. If there is no spouse and no children, the parents take equally. If there are no parents, siblings more remote relatives inherit.

- Definition of spouse rights of common law same sex partners in this field are evolving and should be reviewed carefully. Many provinces now recognize these individuals as potential beneficiaries on intestacy. In Québec, intestacy rules apply only to married

partners or partners who entered into a civil union, which includes same sex partners. In Nova Scotia if two persons register a domestic partner declaration, they will have rights of a spouse for purposes of intestate succession
- Spousal rights on death
  On the death of one spouse. For all provinces, except British Columbia and Prince Edward Island the surviving spouse has a statutory right to elect to claim a division of family property under family law legislation, rather than to take under the will or under the intestacy rules where there is no will.
- Probate matters.
  A grant of probate is a court order that confirms the will as the last will of the deceased and provides the executor with authority to administer an estate.

England & Wales

Intro—For a will to be in valid form, it must be made in accordance with the rules of the country in which the deceased died or domiciled, (habitually resident or a national) at the time the will was executed, or in accordance with the law of the country where it was executed.

Wills—in order to create a valid will or codicil the document must conform to legal requirements and the testator must have the capacity to make a will. The testator must be over the age of 18 years; There are special rules, which apply to a testator in the armed services.

There are specific requirements relating to the validity of wills that can be found in the wills act 1837, as amended including that the will is in writing that, the will is signed by the testator or by some other person in the testators presence and at the testators direction; and the testator intends by signature to give effect to a valid will.

There are also provisions as to attestation regarding how the testator's signature should be made or acknowledged in the presence of two independent witnesses. A testator is required to have the same capacity to revoke a will as to make one.

A will can be revoked voluntarily by the testator, or involuntarily by operation of law. Voluntary revocation can occur in a number of ways for example, by the testators making a later validly executed will or codicil, destroying the original will, or making a written declaration of intention to revoke the will and executing it in accordance with formalities.

Involuntary revocation occurs on the subsequent marriage/formation of civil partnership of the testator unless the previously made will was stated to be made in expectation of the testators intended marriage /formation of civil partnership. There is a presumption that any alterations found in a will were made after it was executed. Any alteration shall be executed as though it were a will, or one of the following must apply, otherwise it will be invalid:

The alterations are initialed or signed by the testator and the attesting witnesses at the time and of the execution of the will.

—The changes are mentioned in the attestation clause of the will or in a separate note at the end of the will, or—the will is republished or re-executed and republished including the alterations. (with alterations included)

Resources

-Books, articles and journals

Tristam and Cootes probate practice.

Butterworth's Wills Probate & Administration, Service

Williams, Williams on Wills

Underhill & Haydon, Law of Trusts & Trustees

Trusts & Estates, Legal Studies Publishing Limited.

United States of America

Most states require that wills be in writing and signed at the end by the testators, who must be of legal age and sound mind at the time of making the will. The testator's signature is to be witnessed by at least two witnesses under most state laws. Many states allow for self proving wills which include affidavits signed by a notary, the testator and the witnesses that can be admitted to probate without the witnesses having to testify in court that the will is valid.

In addition to printed or typewritten wills, some states

Recognize holographic forms of will.

State law provides that a will can be revoked or altered by another will later in date, a writing of the testator clearly indicating an intention to revoke or after the will and executed with the same formalities as a will, or by an act of mutilation or destruction, such as burning or tearing

Under state law children generally have no fixed inheritance rights in the property of a deceased parent, other than in the case of intestacy. Any child may be disinherited as long as the testator has clearly expressed the intent to do so and the entire estate is left to others. Otherwise, the child will be entitled to a share of the intestate estate.

An individual who dies without a valid will is said to have died intestate. Even with a valid will, property not disposed of by that will or by a non-probate arrangement, passes by intestate. Every state has statutory regime identifying the heirs entitled to, and their respective share of, intestate property. If there are no heirs, or existing heirs do not accept the inheritance, any unclaimed property passes to the state.

State law generally protects spouses by restricting the ability to transfer property during lifetime and at death through dower, which is a wife's right to a life estate in real property owned during the marriage, and curtsey, a husband's comparable right.

"Advance directives regarding medical care."

Most states recognize advance directives regarding medical care. State law may provide for living wills detailing the type of medical care that would be accepted or refused in various circumstances and/or health care powers of attorney appointing an agent to make health care decisions in the event that the patient is unable to do so.

"Assets not requiring probate."

Non-probate arrangements, sometimes called will substances, provide for the passage of title on death as specified by state law, joint arrangement, or banking agreement, thereby superseding by state law, joint arrangement, or will. Life insurance is also considered a will substitute when the contract provides that policy proceeds re to be paid to a named beneficiary other than the decedents estate. Under a joint tenancy with right of survivorship co-owners share an equal and undivided interest in the whole of the property. When one owner dies. Title to the property passes to the remaining owners

Australia

The law of wills in Australia is that each jurisdiction in this country has its own statutory provisions. Formalities are an important issue in each jurisdiction.

In general, though the courts grant probate for wills even though the formal requirements are not complied with i.e. weight is placed on the "intent" of the parties . . .

Certain dependants can apply for relief.

There are rules for intestacy (whole or partial

INDIA

Succession: Testate and intestate succession, Where a person dies leaving a will, they are said to have died testate. In the absence of a will, they are said to have died intestate. A will may be oral or in writing. If in writing, it must be signed by the testator and attested by two or more witnesses. The decreased property is called the estate and the inheritors of the estate are called beneficiaries. All the rules and procedures for administration of testamentary succession are stipulated in the Indian succession act, while intestate are under personal laws. Muslims, who are governed under Muslim inheritance law, are subject to forced heir ship rules, which require at least two-thirds of the deceased's estate to be inherited by the line of succession. Apart from Muslims, only residents of the state of Goa are subject to forced heir ship under the Goan law rules. Probate: Probate is the official evidence of the executor's right to represent and dispose of the testator's estate as per the terms of the will under the Indian succession act. Probate can be granted only to an executor appointed under a will, who has to apply the relevant court for the appointment of an executor.

Singapore

The intestate Succession Act governs the distribution of the estate of a non-Muslim intestate descendent. The inheritance Act sets out the circumstances under which the spouse or children of a non Muslim deceased may apply to the court for an order that the estate make provision for the maintenance of the spouse and children. The process of and procedure for obtaining a grant of probate or letters of administration are set out in the Probate and Administration Act in the rules of Court.

Malaysia

The Wills Act 1959 applies to wills by non-Muslims domiciled in Malaysia. The wills ordinance 1953 applies to wills made by non-Muslims domiciled in Sabah. The Inheritance Act 1951 is the principal statute setting out the basis of an application to court for reasonable provision to be made for maintenance of a deceased's spouse or children.

Germany

The test for applicability of the German law of succession for movable and immovable property is nationality, not residence or domicile. Thus the estate of German citizens is generally subject to German law of succession, which also governs distribution. Forced heir ship rules apply to testate succession.

The description of a will in Kenya is basically similar to that in England.

- That all property may be disposed of by will.
- That no will of a person underage is valid
- That two witnesses must be present (at the same time) when witnessing a will.
- That a gift to an attesting witness/or his/her spouse is void.
- That a will, will be revoked by marriage (except where the testator intended that the will should not be revoked e.g. where the testator is expecting to marry a particular person).
- That no will will be revoked otherwise than by another will or codicil or by its destruction.

In general, a will has no effect until the testator dies (13) and a document intended by a person to be his will is usually worded so as to describe itself as a will.

In deciding whether a document can be proved as a will, the court ascertains the intention of the person who executed (from the language and other evidence). It is revocable until death. A testator cannot make a will which is irrevocable during this lifetime. A person can leave only one will (14)

A testator can leave a conditional will (that he intends it to take effect only if some specified condition is satisfied).

A will can appoint a guardian or executor.

One can make a contract to leave a will and two persons can make mutual wills.

A Will has been defined as 'the legal declaration by a person of his wishes or intentions regarding the disposition of his property after his death, made and executed according to certain rules— . . .''

There are differences between a Kenyan will and English will. Here are some of them.

In England only a member of the armed forced or merchant marine during a period of active service can make an oral will.

In England two, witnesses must be present at the same time.

Lastly, in England, the law recognizes no property in the dead body of a human being.

THE MIDDLE EAST

Before we come to a discussion on the Islamic law of wills or inheritance in this region it might be worthwhile discussing what Islamic law, in brief, discussing a few issues which are relevant to inheritance law.

Islam is a religion and a way of life based on the commandment of Allah contained in the Holy Quran, and that in the absence of guidance from the Quran the Hadiths of the prophet, the interpretation of the verses of the Holy Quran by the Sahaaba, will be binding on future generations. [1]

Every Muslim is under an obligation to fashion his/her entire life in accordance with the foregoing. So he has to observe at every step what is right (Halal) and what is wrong (Haram).

Muslim laws consist of a moral, ethical and social code.

It is therefore said to be a complete way of life, in spiritual as well as the economic system and external relations.

Muslim laws cover family relations, crime and punishment, inheritance and disposal of property as well as well as the economic system and external relations.

LOCAL PRONOUNCEMENTS IN KENYA

MUSLIM LAW

In a Nigerian case (1), a deceased Muslim died having written a will in accordance with the Wills Act 1887 of England.

Because he followed the provisions of this Act, he disposed of his property in a manner conflicting with the Quran which allows a Muslim testator to dispose of only 1/3 of his property by way of a will.

(The rest to be disposed of according to rules laid down by the Muslim Sect to which he belonged).

This Will was challenged, and it was held that since he chose to write his will according to the

Wills Act of England, Muslim Law could not apply and English Law as the governing law.

In another case (2). The issue was whether the estate of a deceased member of the Wadigo tribe of the Coast who was Muslim followed Islamic Law or Customary Law of the Wadigo.

The court of Appeal confirmed the view prevalent at the time that Islamic Law prevailed over Customary Law in the Coast.

HINDU LAW

In another case (3), involving Jurisdiction the Plaintiff widow sued the Defendant who was the deceased's only son and who had inherited the entire estate of his father.

She claimed that by virtue of the Hindu Marriage & Divorce Act of 1946 (Ordinance 43) she was entitled to a monthly sum as maintenance out of her husband's estate.

The marriage was contracted out of Kenya and Ordinance provided that a marriage contracted out of Kenya could not be deemed as a valid marriage for the purposes of succession to be valid.

It was therefore held that the widow could not establish any right of succession.

The Law of Succession Act Cap 160 has changed this.

CHAPTER 32

CONCLUSIONS

THE TRUSTS AND ESTATES PRACTITIONER

In an earlier edition I had recommended the need for "wills Practitioners".

Since then I have been a retired member of the worldwide association entitled the Society of Trust and Estates Practitioners. (STEP). They are the leading professional body for the trust and estate profession worldwide.

STEP members come from the legal, accountancy corporate administration banking financial planning insurance and related professions.

Members of STEP include the most experienced and senior practitioners in the fields of trusts and estates.

I have compiled my material on the international scene from the latest STEP Directory and Yearbooks.

STEP was founded in 1991 with the aim of bringing together all the senior practitioners in the various fields and cutting across professional; boundaries. Through meetings, seminars, lectures and the exchange of technical papers and reports, members share information, knowledge and experience and benefit from the network of contacts that memberships provides . . . There is a Council which heads the regional committees based in Australasia and East Asia, Canada and the USA, Caribbean, Celtic, Channel Islands England and Wales Europe Mediterranean, Africa and the Indian Ocean.

STEP is administered from its worldwide offices in Central London by its Chief Executive and experienced team all of whom may be contacted at

Grosvenor Gardens,
London SW1W 0GT
E mail step@step.org
Website http://www.step.org

BURIALS

At present, in England, the law recognizes no property in the dead body of a person. Therefore a testator cannot in theory dispose of his dead body and a direction in will to that effect is void. (1)

The testator appointed in a will is usually entitled to the custody and possession of the dead body and it is his duty to dispose of it as long as there are sufficient funds for it.

Express directions, in the lifetime of a person (either in a will or otherwise), are consequently not enforceable but may have moral force. As a matter of practice a testator needs to ensure that his wishes as to the disposal of his body are quickly brought to the notice of the person in possession of it after his death; in fact a matter of minutes are important if he wants his body parts used for transplant.

It is advisable to, in addition to indicating his intention in his will, advise the executor or leave a letter with the said executor to be opened immediately after his death.

LIVING WILLS

A living will is a directive to doctors, instructing them of ones desire to have life-prolonged measures <u>withheld</u> or <u>withdrawn</u> in the event of a terminal illness.

In the USA it is signed, dated and witnessed with many of the same formalities as a last will and testament. At the time of writing in the USA,

42 states have enacted statutes setting out the requirements for creating a valid living will.

In 1990, the Supreme Court of USA ruled that a state may require clear and convincing evidence of your wishes before permitting the withdrawal of life-prolonging medical procedures. A living will can provide such clear and convincing evidence.

A living will can permit you in the authors view to die with dignity and may spare someone years of comatose existence. Medical technology has achieved a great deal in prolonging lives. But in many cases although life is prolonged there is no way for the person to return to a meaningful and productive life. If one prefers not to live a life that can be prolonged but not improved, a living will lets you inform your physician of this fact.

A living will also serves as a means of protection for doctors, hospitals and family members who must ultimately decide when to withdraw or withhold medical treatment.

If one decides to revoke one's living will, one should attach a copy of the will to the revocation and send it to anyone who received a copy of the living will.

Neither of these provisions has legal status in England yet, although they are encountered by doctors in practice and are given <u>a measure of regard</u> informally when health care decisions are being made about those who have become incompetent.

Elsewhere, places such as in Australia, in the states of South Australia and Victoria have enacted enabling legislation on this issue, as have the Canadian provinces of Nova Scotia and Quebec. As in the United States, there is a variation in the forms and terminology of such provisions of such provisions, although the end result is that of empowering patient self-determination.

Varying degrees of non-legal but formally constituted arrangements are in effect in Switzerland, Germany and Holland.

A common thread in these is the "obligation", imposed by the national professional organization, for doctors to take account of living wills, when they exist, in treating a patient.

These and other examples throughout the world indicate that attempts by patients to influence their future medical care are gradually gaining public recognition.

Another factor is development in medical technology which makes the extension of life beyond its natural span more likely.

Among the simpler of these processes are artificial ventilation, nutrition and hydration, and giving of antibiotics. Finally the advent of HIV and AIDS has brought with it the specter of otherwise healthy young individuals contemplating an untimely and possibly drawn out and painful death.

What is the legal effect of the advance directives? Again, the American example is instructive. The main effect is usually that the directive's existence exempts from any civil or criminal liability a doctor acting according to its terms, — for instance, by withdrawing treatment . . . .

How should the growing interest in advance directive be acted upon in this country?

Self-determination over medical care is such a complex and important matter that it should be legally recognized and regulated by legislation.

It is the authors view that if there is such a stipulation, preferably in writing, the next of kin should endeavor to obtain a court order to authorize the doctor or physician to remove life support systems.

HUMAN GENETIC INTERVENTION

The prevailing global public debate on aspects of cell cloning in humans as well as animals gained urgency in 1997 with the birth of Dolly the sheep in Scotland, the first mammal to be cloned from the frozen cells of another. She was the identical twin of a long dead adult, and gave birth to six lambs, before dying in 2003, after suffering from acute arthritis and a lung infection. This experiment made people think very differently about biology, stem cells, present in small numbers in most organs, are significant because they have the "plasticity to develop into virtually any kind of tissue, especially if the come from embryos, rather than adults whose cells are currently thought to have less plasticity. Those stem cells may be taken from existing embryos or derived from a process of fusing a cell and an egg whose nucleus has been removed. Where cloning is used to foster cell lines that may help crate tissues and organs, it is labeled 'therapeutic"; alternatively, the embryo derived from the fusion of cell and egg may be implanted in a uterus for reproductive cloning, as with dolly the sheep, there are scientists and others who do not find it morally objectionable, most do find it so.

It is becoming the subject of tight regulation in most jurisdictions.

Because there is no property interest in the body, states, in the STEP journal of April 2007, Joshua S. Rubenstein, STEP managing partner at a well know law firm in New York states that gifts of frozen genetic material are technically not included in gifts of one's residuary estate and may not be made by specific bequest. In the matrimonial context, case law has evolved that the right to use frozen genetic material is a question of contract law, and that in the case of disagreement, custody of frozen genetic material is generally to be awarded to the party wishing not to procreate(as the party wishing to procreate generally has other options for doing so).Similarly case law is developing that the right to use frozen genetic material posthumously is to be governed by the contract entered into with the facility providing the assisted productive technology services.

Most jurisdictions have well established bodies of law dealing with the rights of inheritance of individuals conceived prior to but born after death. It is not until quite recently that any jurisdictions have begun to address the inheritance rights of an individual where implantation occurs after the parent's death.

Those jurisdictions that have considered the issues have tended to adopt one of two approaches.

The first is intended to protect the reasonable expectations of the decedent, and provides that in the absence of an express intention to the contrary, individuals implanted after death have no inheritance rights. The second is intended to protect society's interest in the predictable long term administration of estates and trusts, and provide that such individuals must be born within a relatively short time after death-generally two years-in order to have inheritance rights. In the absence of such legislation, however, the ability for posthumous implantation to occur has the potential for unanticipated and frequently irrational results under existing law.

For Example;

- o If a frozen sperm and egg were fertilized and implanted after death, the resulting child might violate the rule against perpetuities, not having been a life in being, even if birth occurred within a year of death. On the other hand, if an embryo were created and frozen during life, and implanted after death, the resulting child might not violate the rule against perpetuities, having been a life in being, even if birth occurred 100 years after death.

- o If a childless terminally ill father had frozen his sperm with the specific intention of permitting his wife to use it after death, but governing law or will required legitimacy in order for a beneficiary to inherit, his resulting child might have no inheritance rights from him. Since conception would have occurred after death, it would have happened when he was not married and the child would be illegitimate
- o Many jurisdictions have after-born child statutes, protecting the gifts of children born after the date a will is executed
- o Family dependency laws might apply to posthumously reproduced childrenThis is clearly an area where developments in medicine have far outpaced developments in law.

Jurisdictions need to consider these issues closely and enact remedial legislation. In the meantime planners need to find out whether clients have participated in assisted reproductive technologies, make sure that the governing contracts to express their intent, and draft what documents we can to address the disposition of their remains and the posthumous use of their genetic material in the manner they intend.

In his book "Muslim Ethics, Emerging Vistas" by Prof Amyn Sajoo, (lecturer in Civil Society and

Islam at Simon Frazer University and media commentator), published by IB Taurus and the Institute of Ismaili Studies www.iis.ac.uk . . . .

(from whom I have borrowed the above eloquent intro to this subject states, again so succinctly,

"A qualified ethical acceptance of therapeutic cloning of stem cells appears to have emerged, not least in the Muslim world with its comparatively permissive stance on early embryonic status. A new stem cell research centre in Saudi Arabia . . . will have the endorsement of fatwas that emphasize the public welfare element in allowing the use of cells taken from miscarried fetuses . . . . However, there are potential grounds for ethical concern about therapeutic cloning).

Stem cells developed for muscle tissue, for instance, may assist therapy for cardiac damage or muscular dystrophy, yet the same process could lend itself for commercial use in boosting muscular or cardiac tissue for elite sportsmen.

A related issue is that of access to biomedical resources within and among societies if there is not to be a "biotech divide" in favour of a privileged few.

As Muslim health professionals and scholars reflect on these questions, the rush of developments in the lab etc only aggravates the issues

THE LAW OF SUCCESSION IN THE MUSLIM WORLD

There are, directly or indirectly 35 verses in the Quran which refer to inheritance (Mirath- inheritance to be divided from the property of the deceased amongst his successors).

The rules relating to inheritance in Islam are based on the principle that the property should devolve on the successors of the deceased based on those who have the strongest claim (by blood or marriage).

The problem is that the deceased may leave more than one person, so related or connected with him so it would be difficult to decide who should get what share.

It is indicated in the Quran "of your parents and sons you do not know which of them are the nearest and of most benefit to you (1)".

According to Islamic law, therefore, the estate is distributed among the claimants in such order or proportion as were most in harmony with the natural strength of their claims.

In the period before Islam, the rules of inheritance excluded both women and children because according to the tribes living then, only those who could go to the battlefield would inherit.

As far as women were concerned, she was considered to be the property of the husband's family and so could not inherit.

A strict warning is given to those who are in charge of disposing of and dividing up an estate. They are asked to observe the principles of justice and to be kind and helpful (2).

The above injunction from the Quran has four legal implications:

- The inheritance is not meant for men only but women also have the right to inherit
- The property left behind by a deceased however little it might be, must be distributed jointly amongst the heirs.
- Islamic law of inheritance applies to all kinds of property, moveable or immovable.
- Inheritance matters only arise if the deceased has left any property. If property has been left, however small it must be distributed jointly amongst the heirs.
- Nearer relatives precludes distant relative from inheritance.

There are 3 conditions of inheritance which must be satisfied:

1. The death of the owner of the estate

This must be actual and clear either by real death or by court decree.

It must be proved that there are heirs surviving at the time of death before they are allowed to inherit.

2. In the case of an embryo, it will not inherit unless born alive.

According to a Hadith (3), only one third of the net estate of the deceased is distributable according to the wishes of the deceased, and is so divided.

The balance (i.e. 2/3) is distributed, depending on which sect the Muslim belongs. Volumes have been written on how this 2/3 should be distributed and so it is not within the scope of this book but here is a brief outline of how the property of two Groups devolve are carried out.

According to Hanafi Law there are three kinds of heirs:-

Sharers: They are entitled to a fixed share of the inheritance.

Residuaries: The heirs do not take shares but succeed to the residue left after the claims of the "Sharers" have been satisfied.

Distant kindred: They are all those relations by blood who are neither sharers nor residuaries.

An illegitimate child inherits from his or her mother.

According to the Ithna Ashari Law of inheritance; there are two main classes of heirs:

- Sabab or special clause (legal relationship or marriage)
- Nasab or blood relationship

There are special rules as to how these groups and sub groups inherit but this is outside the scope of this book.

All Muslims generally agree that a murderer or killer shall not inherit from his/her victim.

Also, where sexes differ, the principle that the male gets double the share of the female is followed in both systems.

Modern thinkers and jurists would today view this differently but at that time it was a great stride for the emancipation of women.

After all, women were emancipated only in the recent past in the Western wor

THE ADMINISTRATION OF THE ESTATE OF A DECEASED MUSLIM

Distribution is carried out after the payment of debt "and other right of Allah and his servant"

Normal debt means the debts that are not secured or specifically attached to the estate.

Funeral expenses must also be paid as part of the debts but Islam preaches simplicity, particularly so when one dies. Therefore funeral expenses have to be reasonable.

After taking out the debt (including funeral expenses) the "will" will be carried out. This includes all the gifts that are made during the "death-sickness" of the deceased. The majority of jurists consider them as wills.

As indicated, according to a Hadith of the prophet, however, both wills and such gifts must not exceed one third of the estate of the deceased unless consented to by the heirs.

It has been held that in the Indian subcontinent (4) that since the estate devolves on the heirs at the moment of death, the heirs are at liberty to divide it at any time after death and each heir is liable for the debts of the deceased to the extent only of a share of the debt proportional to the heirs share of the estate.

The right to administer the estate of the deceased Muslim belongs to his executor appointed by his will, failing this, by the person to whom letters of administration are granter by a competent court.

The executor must be a sane adult who must be trustworthy.

WILLS

After taking out the funeral expenses and debts i.e. the debts of the right of Allah and that of individuals, the "Wasiyyah" or the will will be carried out.

The Wasiyyah includes all the gifts that are made during the death-sickness of the deceased (the majority of jurists consider the later also as wills.)

The amount in the above wills and gifts must not, as indicated, exceed one third of the estate of the deceased unless consented to by the heirs.

Every Muslim of sound mind (who is not a minor) may make a will to dispose of his property to the extent permitted by Muslim law.

Under Shia law, if a person has taken poison etc in order to commit suicide and then make a "will", it will not be valid, for those who take a benefit under the will and who have been instrumental in preparing the will, the onus is upon such persons of showing the validity of the transaction (see undue influence and suspicious Circumstances Chapter 4).

Muslim law does not prescribe any form of the will. Such a will need not even be in writing but the intentions of the deceased must be clear and specific and where the disposition is expressly stated to take effect in death, then it is a valid will (see Formalities chapter 5).

When more than one-third of the property has been bequeathed to a stranger, the bequest would be valid only to the extent of one-third of the estate.

Only the heir of a Muslim can object to the excess of disposition.

According to Shia law a bequest of more than one-third of the estate would be valid if all the legal heirs consent to it, either during the lifetime of the testator or after his death. Under Sunni law, the consent of the legal heir to any such bequest must be given after the death of the testator to be valid.

The consent of the legal heirs is to be given by them in person, on attaining majority.

According to Sunni law, if a legatee is not in existence at the time of the death of the death of the testator, the legacy lapses and forms part of the testator's estate.

Under Shia law, the legacy in such cases passes to the other heirs of the deceases, but if there are no such heirs then it passes back to the estate of the deceased (see LEGACIES AND DEVISES, AND THEIR FAILURE)

A Muslim will does not, according to Islamic law, need probate. The estate of the deceased vest in the executor from the date of death of the deceased.

It has been held in the Indian sub continent that the executor of a Muslim will need not be a Muslim. (11)

(1)Quran Chapter 4:11
(2)Quran Chapter 4:7
(3)A Hadith Narrated by said Bin Abi Waqqas
(4)Pirthipal Singh V Husaini Jan (1832)—Bom
(5)8 Bom p 241

292

LIVING WILLS and "assisted suicides" in Islam.

Assisted suicides (euthanasia) is treated as suicide on the part of the individual with no reprieve on grounds of medical necessity. The Islamic Code of Medical Ethics holds that a physician "shall not take away life even when motivated by mercy", basing itself on Prophetic guidance against suicide.

Where a medical condition reduces the body to a vegetative state or medical intervention is otherwise deemed futile, the same principle of sanctity/dignity allows for treatment to cease and life to lapse. Again according to the same code, the physician must recognize his limits as upholder of life, and may desist from "heroic measures' or other passive preservation of the patient (4B)

THE KADHIS' COURTS

The Kadhis court shall have and exercise jurisdiction on matters of Muslim law relating to personal status, marriage, divorce or inheritance in proceedings in which all the parties profess the Muslim religion (7).

The law and rules of evidence to be applied in a Kadhis' court shall be those applicable under Muslim law subject to certain provisos e.g. no discrimination of witnesses on grounds of religion, sex etc and credibility of a witness will have more importance than number.

The Kadhis court shall keep such records of proceedings and submit returns of proceedings to the high court as directed by the chief justice from time to time.

Lastly the Chief Justice may make rules of the court providing for the procedure on practice to be followed in Kadhis court.

---

1. Sharia: The Islamic Law—By Abdul Rahman P.46

2. ISLAMIC LAW AND INTERNATIONAL COMMERCIAL ARBITRATION BY VK NATHAN-ARBITRATION MAY 1993 (UK)

3. Introduction to Muslim Laws by Y Justice R C Valiani

4.Aziz Bano Muhammad (1925—India)

Hamira Bibi V Zubaida Bibi India

4.B Prof amyn b. Sajoo in "Muslim Ethics, emerging Vistas" (www.iis.org

CHAPTER 33

DIFFERENT BRANCHES OF ISLAMIC LAW

There are two main branches of Muslim law, the Sunni and the Shia.

There are four Sunni subschools or Sub branches, they are the Hanafis, the Malikis, the Shafees and the Hanibees. Since most of the Sunnis belong to the Hanafi school, the presumption is that a Sunni is governed by Hanafi law according to courts both in India and Pakistan.

Shias are divided into three main groups, Bohora, Itha Ashari and Ismaili. Muslim law applicable to each sect or subsect is to prevail. A Sunni woman contracting marriage with a Shia does not thereby become subject to the Shia law and vice versa.

In order to hold that a person is a Sunni or Shia Muslim, it is sufficient for a court to be satisfied with the declaration of such person in respect of his sect of subject.

ARBITRATION

Arbitration is a method of resolution of disputes alternative to the court system.

Such forms of dispute resolution are in the use in the UK and in Kenya and are governed by statutory provisions in both countries. Arbitration in different forms is also practiced in various other countries like the United States and Japan.

Resolution of dispute by arbitration is said to be fast, inexpensive, and utilizes the expertise of the arbitrator who is appointed by the joint agreement of both parties. It is also informal (does not necessarily require the representation of advocates as in the courts of law). The disputes are resolved without the presence of the press so there is no publicity as in the case of court disputes. Decisions of the arbitrator are recognized because they are governed by the Arbitration Acts of Kenya and UK respectively.

In the Arab world the prevalence of the arbitral method of dispute resolution dates to the pre—Islamic era when they were used to settling various squabbles.

Institutionalized and more formal methods were adopted in the market place by traders, and in the regulation of aspects of one's personal life by the pagan priests.

Arbitration was subject to much abuse during this era. It, probably explains pointed references to "Hakamyat" (Arabic for arbitration) in the Quran which established the prophet as the supreme arbitral authority having universal and unlimited jurisdiction. Even after the passing of the prophet, arbitration because of its religious connotations has greater meaning to the Arab countries than litigation in a court of law (2).

A lot of disputes on inheritance matters are resolved by arbitration in the Muslim world.

THE TRUST

Most people understand the importance of a will but comparatively know less about trusts.

A will is a legal document where assets devolve upon your heirs at death. A trust does the same thing. A will names an executor to distribute those assets. A trust names a trustee to do the same thing.

But the main differences are:

A will takes effect when you die. A trust can be set up and used to manage your assets during your lifetime.

The executor of a will can only distribute your assets to your heirs. With a trust, you can give the trustee powers to continue handling your funds long after your death. A will is a public record while a trust provides total privacy from say, inquisitive neighbors, relatives receiving no inheritance and even a conman.

A trust can be useful to provide protection for a handicapped child or disabled relative. A trust can also be useful to a married person planning to leave an inheritance to children from a prior marriage. A trust can also be set up for religious or charitable purposes and relieve yourself of managing your assets.

The origins of trusts in the west can be traced back to the time of the Crusades when warrior knights would entrust their property to the local bishop while they were away fighting. If the knight failed to return, the bishop would be responsible for caring for his widow and children.

Muslim law since the prophet has recognized the creation of a "Waqf" which is many ways similar to a trust.

298

The main differences between a Trust and a Waqf are: (3)

TRUST	WAQF
1. No particular motive is necessary as long as it is legal	1. Generally has to have a pious, charitable or religious motive
2. The originator of the trust himself is a beneficiary.	2. The Waqf cannot reserve any benefit for himself except under Hanafi Law.
3. It may be for any lawful object	3. The ultimate object must be some benefit of mankind.
4. The property vests in the trustee	4. The property is said to vest in Allah.
5. A trustee has larger powers only as a "Manager".	5. The Mutwalli is than a mutwalli
6. It is not necessary that a trust be perpetual, irrevocable or inalienable	6. A Waqf is perpetual, irrevocable and inaliable
7. It reverts back for the benefits of the founder if incapable of execution.	7. The property has to be applied to some other pious, charitable or religious cause

A Waqf can be created in a will just as a trust can be created in a will.

The executor of a Muslim's 'will' automatically becomes a Mutwalli.

A Waqf created by a will without the consent of the rightful heirs is effective only to the extent of one third of the net estate of the Waqf.

If the mode of succession to the office of the Mutwalli is not defined in the will, the mutwalli for the time being is empowered to appoint his own successor by "will".

A Mutwalli may be removed by a competent court on the grounds of untrustworthiness as well as for gross incompetence or misapplication or misuse of the income.

The only requirement for the creation of a Waqf is a clear intention to create the Waqf and the appointment of a Mutwalli. It may be oral or in writing.

EQUITY

In the UK, in the previous centuries, if the courts were too harsh in their rulings, the aggrieved subject could go to the crown (King or Queen) who was considered the Fountain of Justice" for redress. The crown or later the chancellor could make a ruling which was most in accordance with justice, equity and good conscience.

Subsequently courts of equity were established to handle such matters.

The rules of equity and equitable consideration commonly recognized in the courts in England and Kenya are not foreign to the Muslim system but are in fact often referred to and invoked in the adjudication of the cases under the Muslim system. (4)

The field of Islamic law involves a lifetime of study and this topic is only a cursory glance to perk ones interest in this vast, fascinating subject. Please see www.iis.org and authors like professor Amy Sajoo and Dr Mohamed Keshavjee. I have benefited lots, in my little way from these scholars.

APPENDIX
FOREWORD

S. AMOS WAKO, EBS, EGH, MP
ATTORNEY GENERAL

(Relating to my book A Background to wills
and Trusts in Kenya—ISBN 141208036-3 Trafford
Publishing)

I have had the pleasure of reading through this
book on background to Wills in Kenya and have
found it most illuminating especially because
of the author's gallant efforts to explore a subject
least written about in this country.

Little has been written on probate practice
since and before the enactment of the Law
of Succession Act. This book therefore acts as
a watershed on a topic mostly, if not all the
time, treated with awe. It is a simple analytical
restatement of the basic legal principles both
on substantive and practical probate law in
accordance with the provisions of the Law of
Succession Act. Such vital practical aspects in
probate practice as the mode of execution and
revocation of wills including validity thereof are

covered including most contentious subject on dependency.

The book is dotted with hallmark court decisions reproduced in simple form to assist any reader. That the author has had mostly to rely on reported case law from outside this country illustrates the need to develop authoritative coded case law based on local legislations taking into account local circumstances. After all, case law is the principle ingredient of probate practice. Nevertheless, the author has managed to put across the message about the vitality and complexity of probate law and practice as is demonstrated by his attempt to tackle a subject as intricate as perpetuities. Whilst briefly tackling this very demanding topic of validity of dispositions, the author makes a curious reader understand the future need for a greater in-depth analysis of this topic.

In a subject as complex in language and construction as probate law, the author has meticulously used concise simple language with constant fluency that any reader interested in this important subject will find the book worth reading and educative. The book's most poignant message is that one must make a Will and not only a Will but a valid Will for the sake of posterity. I endorse this message and concur with the author's introductory statement that, and I quote, "the cost of a Will is not high, especially compared with headache and confusion that may be caused after your death if you leave no Will or a badly drafted Will". The level of our development and the changing social, cultural and traditional systems will make it imperative that we develop a habit of making Wills.

Whilst a Will need not be in any prescribed format, it is my hope that future publications on this subject will be supplemented with a sample of demonstrative wills for greater practical clarity. Though it is not mandatory to consult a lawyer while making a valid Will, the author has highlighted, and rightly so, the necessity of seeking proper legal advice to ensure adequate guidance and thus avoid resulting pitfalls of subjecting a Will to protracted litigated construction suits.

I recommend the reading of this book to all legal practitioners mainly as a handy guide on day to day ordinary probate business. That the author has spent a considerable time on the subject of Muslim Law of Succession, practitioners and even those on the bench may find this book a worthwhile practical guide in this area. The book is in my considered view a mandatory reading for all those studying law either at the university level or at the Kenya School of Law and including those taking non legal courses containing selected legal syllabus. The disciples of gender rights including our legal legislators may also find this book helpful in understanding ordinary issues relating to the Law of Succession in this country.

SIGNED

S. AMOS WAKO, EBS, EGH, MP

ATTORNEY GENERAL